Augustine of Canterbury

Augustine of Canterbury

Leadership, Mission and Legacy

Robin Mackintosh

www.augustineofcanterbury.org

CANTERBURY
PRESS
Norwich

© Robin Mackintosh 2013

First published in 2013 by the Canterbury Press Norwich
Editorial office
108–114 Golden Lane,
London, EC1Y 0TG

Canterbury Press is an imprint of Hymns Ancient and Modern Ltd
(a registered charity)
13A Hellesdon Park Road, Norwich,
Norfolk, NR6 5DR, UK

www.canterburypress.co.uk

British Library Cataloguing in Publication data

A catalogue record for this book is available
from the British Library

978 1 84825 534 0

Typeset by Manila Typesetting Company
Printed and bound in Great Britain by
Ashford Colour Press Ltd, Gosport, Hampshire

Contents

Preface

This book explores key events in the sixth century that shaped the future of England. The story of Augustine's mission to England, sent by Gregory the Great of Rome in 596, still has relevance today. The book is written for theology students training for ordained and Reader ministries and for clergy looking for insights into leadership, spirituality and mission from our roots in England's earliest mission. It is also accessible to the many non-specialists who are drawn to historical themes and characters of earlier periods in Western Europe generally and the history of England in particular.

The account of Augustine's mission brings together insights from recent historical, archaeological and sociological studies that have a bearing on both Augustine's mission and context in the world of Late Antiquity, Anglo-Saxon England and sub-Roman Britain. While the body of academic research and writing continues to grow concerning the events surrounding the period of the Augustinian mission to Kent in 596–7, much less attention has been devoted to the story of Augustine the person, and even less to the leadership he exercised in mounting a mission to the Anglo-Saxon people or to the monastic spirituality that energized the enterprise.

The implications of Augustine's mission for leadership and spirituality range from events in Rome through France to England as we consider the complex political journey through Merovingian France and the outcomes in Anglo-Saxon Kent and in the west of Britain. Critical issues of leadership and spirituality are considered as we evaluate Augustine's legacy as the first Archbishop of Canterbury.

Introduction

There is a growing body of writing concerning the periphery of the Augustinian mission to Kent in AD 596–7; however, much less attention has been devoted to the leadership that Augustine exercised, the nature and development of his mission to the Anglo-Saxon people, or the spirituality that energized this enterprise. Most studies leave Canterbury's first archbishop too deeply obscured in the shadow of Gregory the Great for his own contribution to be clearly seen. This book explores the events that led to Augustine's mission and how it was carried out, the immediate outcomes in Kent and Augustine's attempts to build a bridge to the British Church. Critical leadership issues are considered as they arose at each stage of the mission. The spirituality that energized the mission is assessed.

A second aim is to bring together insights from recent historical, archaeological and sociological studies that have a bearing on both Augustine's mission and context in the world of Late Antiquity, Anglo-Saxon England and sub-Roman Britain. It might be possible to uncover a more coherent narrative relating to Augustine's mission so that Augustine's own role and contribution can emerge more clearly. This could also make richer and wider use of existing material in imaginative ways for exploring implications for our present generation.

This leads to a third aim – to recover insights into the inner spiritual 'DNA' of Augustine's leadership-for-mission and consider what implications this might have for the Church in the twenty-first century.

A final purpose is to challenge the basis for a negative interpretation of both Augustine and his contribution to the Kentish mission itself. This begins with, but is not restricted to, Bede. To what extent is a negative stance justified? The revival of interest in things 'Celtic 'in the last 100 years has cast almost any discourse relating to Augustine as self-evidently 'Roman, bad; Celtic, good'; Augustine 'austere and hierarchical'; Aidan and Cuthbert 'world-affirming and non-hierarchical'; the Synod of Whitby, a triumph for Wilfrid the 'Romanizer' but a disaster for the Church in Northumbria and particularly for 'Celtic Christianity'. That these discourses are still played out more than 1400 years after the events themselves is regrettable, and the underlying discourses at the least need re-examination.

The Venerable Bede (c. 673–735)

Almost everything we know about Augustine comes from or through Bede, a Northumbrian born after the Synod of Whitby in 664, and the letters of Pope Gregory the Great, who commissioned Augustine for the mission to the *Angli*. Bede as a young boy entered the monastery of Monkwearmouth-Jarrow, established by a Northumbrian nobleman, Benedict Biscop. Biscop travelled extensively on the Continent assembling a superb library, not only for his own monastery, but also for Saint Augustine's Abbey in Canterbury. In contrast, Bede travelled no more than a few miles from Jarrow during his lifetime, his considerable breadth of scholarship nurtured initially by Biscop's library and other books and manuscripts that were sent to him for his studies. These included accounts from Albinus, Abbot at Canterbury, and Nothelm, a priest and later Archbishop of Canterbury (735–9), who journeyed to Rome and copied some of Gregory's papal correspondence relating to Augustine's mission. Nothelm visited Bede twice at Jarrow-Wearmouth, before and after his journey to Rome.

Bede's Preface to *The Ecclesiastical History of the English People* records that Albinus (d. 733), Abbot of Saint Augustine's

Abbey and educated by both Abbot Hadrian and Archbishop Theodore, had in the early decades of the eighth century:

> carefully ascertained, from written records or from the old traditions, all that the disciples of St Gregory had done in the kingdom of Kent or in the neighbouring kingdoms. He passed on to me whatever seemed worth remembering through Nothelm, a godly priest of the Church in London, either in writing or by word of mouth. Afterwards Nothelm went to Rome and got permission from the present Pope Gregory (II) to search through the archives of the holy Roman Church and there found some letters of St Gregory and of other popes. On the advice of Father Albinus he brought them to us on his return to be included in our History.[1]

Bede's purpose in writing substantially shaped the discourse through which he presented and interpreted Augustine's mission. Bede saw himself as a direct beneficiary of the Christian mission to the Anglo-Saxons begun in 597, and he knew at first hand the struggle to bring Christianity to pagan Saxons and peace to warring English kingdoms. His greatest project, in conjunction with Abbot Eadfrith of Lindisfarne, was to bring about reconciliation between the English kingdoms. Bede's *magnum opus* was completed around 731, a mid-point between Augustine's mission to Kent and Alfred the Great as King of the English people.

Bede's gratitude to Gregory the Great for the mission to England was deeply felt. He wrote of Gregory:

> We can and should by rights call him our apostle, for though he held the most important see in the whole world and was head of Churches which had long been converted to the true faith, yet he made our nation, till then enslaved to idols, into a Church of Christ.[2]

Bede's *Ecclesiastical History* was more than a chronicle of events; it was intended to shape the future as a companion-piece to Abbot Eadfrith's monumental work, the Lindisfarne Gospels. Both were created to inspire a vision for one nation, united under God. Bede's central message in his *Ecclesiastical History of the English People* explains why this was so. Before the coming of Augustine the Anglo-Saxons were divided into warring pagan kingdoms; after the coming of Christianity, there was one 'English people', a Christian nation substantially at peace within itself. The gospel had proved mightier than the sword. Jesus prayed to the Father for his disciples so that 'they may be one, as we are one', and the Psalmist exclaims, 'How very good it is when brothers and sisters live together in unity!'[3]

When Bede wrote his words of acclaim for Gregory, England was not yet a nation in any meaningful sense; that still lay in the future under Alfred the Great. Bede's work helped create a climate that brought a person of Alfred's character to the fore, and he became the first ruler who could be called 'the King of the English people'.

Bede's Portrayal of Augustine

Bede consciously downplays Augustine's achievements in the mission to the English by emphasizing instead the role of Gregory the Great. This becomes evident in the questions, stated or implied, over Augustine's leadership of the mission. Four key issues, usually identified as raising doubts over Augustine's leadership, are explored in this text:

- *The false start to Augustine's mission:* was this due to Gregory's lack of preparation, or Augustine's failure to exercise 'firm leadership' in dealing with his rebellious monks?
- *Augustine's letter to Gregory:* by seeking the pope's advice on church matters, was this hesitancy or weakness on Augustine's part in the face of multiple challenges, or alternatively does this indicate a lack of briefing in Gregory's preparations for the mission?

- *Augustine's performance of miracles:* did he demonstrate spiritual immaturity and weakness of character?
- *Augustine's failure to win over the British bishops:* was this a clear indication of Augustine's lack of humility or of Gregory's lack of ecumenical vision for a re-established British Church? Or something else entirely?

The political influence of the new religion that Bede looked back to in Augustine's mission was considerable, especially in the inter-relationships between the various Anglo-Saxon kingdoms. At the time of Augustine's mission, the Anglo-Saxons were not yet a coherent people possessing a sense of their own national identity. The spread of Christianity from the end of the sixth century onwards had a profound impact on Anglo-Saxon society as a whole. Augustine and his missionaries, working hand in hand with the Kentish King Aethelberht and his Christian queen, helped pave the way for greater political ties and trade by linking the Anglo-Saxons to a system that was essentially Mediterranean-orientated and city-based. This wider Christian world provided a new set of values and an intellectual climate in which ideas and ideologies could flourish.[4] By 700, Lindisfarne had come round to the Easter dating of the Roman Church, a major issue needing reconciliation. It had also moved closer to the style of more corporate and communal monasticism apparently favoured by Monkwearmouth and Jarrow.[5]

Eadfrith's Lindisfarne Gospels and Bede's *Ecclesiastical History* bring together crucial history and powerful imagery: the prayers of Bertha for the conversion of the Anglo-Saxons are answered, the ecclesial openness of Gregory I is affirmed, the early setbacks of Augustine in failing to create an Ecclesia Britannica are overcome, the labours of Theodore in forging a coherent and ordered English Church bear fruit, Cuthbert's reconciliation of Irish and Roman ecclesiastical and monastic differences after Whitby in 664 unites the community, and through a concerted effort involving Bede's scholarship and Bishop Eadfrith's iconography the vision is realized of a united

English Church and 'English people'. Bede's *Life of St Cuthbert*, Eadfrith's Lindisfarne Gospels and Bede's *Ecclesiastical History of the English People* are foundation stones in this single purpose.

Their work was finished scarcely a moment too soon. The Vikings had already begun their seasonal raids on the British coastline, initially small raids on vulnerable outposts, but soon escalating to outright invasion and wide-scale occupation. In 731 the ultimate roadblock to Danish ambitions still lay more than a century ahead, in the person of Alfred the Great.

Sources for the Mission to Kent

There is very little first-hand information and very few eyewitness reports for Augustine's mission to Kent. The only contemporary sources that relate directly to it are some letters from the Papal *Regesta* of Gregory the Great. Gregory was informed by first-hand reports from Augustine and two of his close companions, the priest Laurentius and the monk Peter who returned briefly to Rome in 598 or 601. They may have carried with them the only letter directly attributed to Augustine, and returned with the pope's detailed response, which is cited in full by Bede.

Augustine's letter to the pope makes no mention of their earlier journey through Francia. Nor does Bede, apart from one episode that seems to have challenged Augustine's leadership at an early stage in the mission. Bede also drew on two contemporary Canterbury sources for his knowledge of the mission, Albinus and Nothelm, but neither of these, as is the case with Augustine's own letter, survives independently of Bede's *Ecclesiastical History*.

Bede's chronology of events relating to Augustine's mission is not always clear or reliable, and this is part of the challenge of determining an authoritative canon of events, their sequence and dates. There is very little expectation of fresh contemporary sources emerging 1400 years after the events that deal directly with Augustine and his mission. What we can hope for are fresh perspectives from several disciplines that throw light on how we might interpret what we already know.

The search for the hidden parts of Augustine's story is helped considerably in that many of the places familiar to Augustine in 596–7 are still in existence and still accessible. These include Gregory's own monastery of Gregorio Magno in Rome, which survives as a Carmelite monastery with a seventeenth-century reconstruction only one layer or so above Gregory's original family home. Also Ostia Antica, the ancient Port of Rome, continues to be excavated, revealing a remarkably preserved city much as Augustine of Canterbury would have known it. In France the baptistery at Aix existed in the sixth century and remains intact, and the cathedral at Arles also retains its early features. The caves at Saint Martin's Marmoutier monastery are still accessible, as are Saint-Denis and Saint-Germain-des-Prés churches but not their monastic buildings.

In England, within a mile or so of the shores of Kent, the crumbling walls of the ancient Roman fort of Richborough still stand, and the beach where Augustine allegedly first met Aethelberht is preserved beneath the rolling turf of, appropriately, Saint Augustine's Golf Course, owned by the Dean and Chapter of Canterbury Cathedral. The site (but none of the ruins) of the ancient fishing village of Sandwic, precursor to present-day Sandwich, is still accessible a few hundred yards from the quay on the River Stour. The city of Canterbury itself is still surrounded by its Roman wall for nearly half of its perimeter, following the same boundary that was familiar to the first missionaries. Saint Martin's Church, dedicated by Queen Bertha on a hillside overlooking the city and still in a remarkable state of preservation, continues as the oldest place of worship continuously in use in England. Combined with the ruins of Saint Augustine's Abbey and the present Cathedral, Saint Martin's is also part of a recognized World Heritage Site.

These are among the remaining physical reminders of Augustine's mission, still evident 1400 years after his death, and through which the pope's missioner might yet emerge more clearly from Gregory's shadow into a light of his own.

Notes

1 Bede, *Ecclesiastical History of the English People*, Oxford: Oxford World Classics, 1999, p. 3, subsequently Bede, *Ecclesiastical History*.
2 Bede, *Ecclesiastical History* II.1.
3 Alan Thacker, 'Bede and History', in Scott DeGregorio (ed.), *The Cambridge Companion to Bede*, Cambridge: Cambridge University Press, 2010, p. 185.
4 Lloyd and Jennifer Laing, *Britain's European Heritage*, Stroud: Sutton Publishing Ltd, 1995, p. 185.
5 Michelle Brown, *How Christianity Came to Britain and Ireland*, Oxford: Lion Publishing, 2006.

PART I

The Launch of Augustine's Mission

PART II

The Launch of Augustine's Mission

Rome and Empire

In the 14th year of the reign of Emperor Maurice Tiberius, Pope Gregory the Great, last of a line of theologians known as the Latin Fathers, launched a mission to re-found the Catholic Church on English soil. The circumstances of the time made this an unusually bold and risky enterprise. Sixth-century Italy was a society in turmoil, in many respects in no position to launch an evangelistic mission to a remote island at the northwestern edge of the known world. The days of grand empire lay behind; the emperors had not lived in Rome for 200 years.[1]

The Decline of Rome

Constantine had built his new capital in 330, and in 402 the Western Emperor Honorius had moved his court away from Rome to Ravenna on the northeast coast of Italy. The last Western Emperor Augustulus abdicated in 476 after considerable pressure from the Roman Senate, who assured Zeno the Eastern Emperor that 'the majesty of a sole monarch is sufficient to pervade and protect, at the same time, both the East and the West'. Their letter effectively ended the Western Empire, so that until the fifteenth century the Byzantine emperors administered the affairs of Empire from the comparative safety of Constantinople.

In contrast, Roman society in these last days of Latin Antiquity was in sharp decline. However, the end of Late Antiquity came suddenly and unexpectedly when in 602 the Roman army on the Danube frontier mutinied, and Maurice was dethroned as Emperor. From the 540s until the mid-eighth century, the Bubonic Plague was a constant factor in the world of Late Antiquity, particularly in the West, so that there was no decade in these two centuries when the plague was not inflicting death somewhere in the Mediterranean region.[2]

By 590 Italy, stricken internally by famine and plague, was laid waste externally by Germanic Lombard invasions. Milan in the north and Rome in the south lay in ruins. Two spearheads pressed further south, creating the duchies of Spoleto north of Rome and Benevento to the south, where the invasion came to a halt. This time Rome did not fall, but the city was swamped with refugees. Benedictine monks from Monte Cassino also fled to Rome, as did some 3000 nuns. The food shortage became critical, and one of Gregory's first tasks after he became pope in 590 was to secure grain supplies from Sicily. This required considerable sums of money to alleviate suffering.

Monasteries

By the launch of Augustine's mission in 596, Rome itself had been under siege for much of the sixth century. The old aristocracy had fled from the onslaught, and few had returned. A leisured class no longer existed to pursue the traditions of a literary culture; monastic communities ringing the Mediterranean had begun to take their place. One of these, Iles de Lérins (*Lerinus*) on the Côte D'Azur, received widespread recognition for its leading role in a newly emerging intellectual world and for providing some of the leading bishops of post-Roman Gaul. In contrast to the comparative peace enjoyed at Saint-Honorat on the southern coast of Provence, blockades, destruction, depopulation and famine were commonplace in Rome throughout Gregory's lifetime. At its zenith, Rome had boasted a million inhabitants; by the end of the sixth century the population had shrunk to little more than 20,000. All the same, pilgrims flocked to Rome in thousands to pray at the shrines of the early saints, particularly Saint Peter and Saint Paul.[3]

The Roman Church

The survival of the Roman Church in the sixth century was by no means a foregone conclusion. Catholicism was no longer the dominant religious force of the Empire. The Lombard invaders were Arians and not well disposed towards Catholicism. They were bought-off at a staggering cost with tribute to keep them from attacking Rome. Nearly all of the funds came from the dwindling resources of the Church, comprising the 'Patrimony of Peter', landed estates gifted to the Church over the centuries in particular, and which stretched from North Africa through much of Western Europe. Gregory's major innovation was efficient management of this heritage through dividing the Patrimony into 15 sections, each administered by a Rector appointed by Gregory himself.

The papal chancery or *Regesta* for holding and authenticating documents, including land ownership records and increasingly foreign relations, was originally staffed by 19 deacons, but increased several times over under Gregory as new ranks were created – subdeacons, treasurers, notaries and senior executive officers, comprising the largest civil service outside of Constantinople.

The Lateran Palace would have seethed with people coming and going on papal business to all parts of what once comprised the Roman Empire.[4] However, the Lateran was remote from major concentrations of the Roman population which clustered near the three remaining bridges spanning the Tiber. As the Lateran Basilica did not contain the actual relics of Saint John, it lacked the pilgrimage drawing-power of the basilicas of Saint Peter or Saint Paul. It would take until the twelfth century for the Lateran Basilica to be firmly established on the itinerary of pilgrims to Rome.[5]

Pope Gregory's relationship with the Emperor Maurice further compounded matters for the Western Church, already strained by disagreements concerning the Patriarch of Constantinople. By the late sixth century, the Mediterranean was ringed by patriarchates of the Orthodox Church, leaving the Church of Rome increasingly isolated. The prospects for schism were increasing. From Gregory's perspective, the only path for the expansion of the Catholic faith now lay to the northwest, in places where even the Byzantine legions had no power to go.

Late Antiquity at the Close of the Sixth Century

The wider world into which Augustine was about to lead his group was a mixture of both continuity and discontinuity with the Roman past. In terms of legacy, the Romans had supplied the building blocks for political, social and cultural practice in every post-Roman society throughout the sixth and into the seventh century. Post-imperial kings drew heavily on great themes from the Roman past, presenting themselves as triumphant military commanders in the late Roman fashion.

Gregory's ideals were ecclesiastical rather than Roman, and he had little interest in quarrying the Empire's past.[6] In Francia, the Merovingian kings cultivated a complex political ideology that also looked to the Roman past, as did their government structures.[7] The material and status rewards of maintaining links with the Roman Church and the Byzantine Empire were hugely attractive. The Emperor Maurice and Pope Gregory were both well aware of this, and both played them to full advantage.

All the post-Roman societies, whether pagan, Christian or, by the middle of the seventh century, Muslim, were habituated to violence, which was exercised particularly by powerful kings, nobles and their retainers. Throughout much of Augustine's journey from Rome to Canterbury, the potential threat of violence would remain a concern for his party. A warrior culture meant weapons, and weapons carried by young men brought problems. Clergy were expressly forbidden to carry weapons, and this would also apply to Augustine and his monks for whom protection was a matter of faith rather than military prowess.

Slavery

The slave trade was ubiquitous in this as in earlier periods and about to become much more widespread by the mid-seventh century with the expansion of Slavic fur-trade networks. Little concern was expressed for the practice of slavery and those caught in its web. Slaves were accepted as part of the familia, but in the role of unfree domestic servants.[8] The distinction between slave and freeman, as Rowan Williams points out, has its roots in the ancient world of Greece and Rome:

> A citizen is someone whose choices and destiny are not owned by someone else. And a citizen therefore is someone who has a voice in the community, who is protected as an individual by the law and who can in some significant degree decide the circumstances of their personal life. A slave is someone who enjoys none of those privileges. A slave is someone who does not have a voice in public decision-making, who does not have protection by law, whose circumstances are decided by someone else.[9]

There is little sign that slavery was regarded as morally wrong by most Christians, despite Christianity's explicit egalitarianism in Paul's 'neither Jew nor Greek, neither slave nor free . . .'.[10] Some did challenge the prevailing practices. Bede records that Pope Gregory bought the freedom of two Anglo-Saxon boys from the slave market in Rome, while the pope's *Regesta* records a letter from the pope giving instructions for two English boys, formerly slaves, to receive a monastic education in Francia.[11]

Corruption

Much of the post-Roman world was deeply corrupt. Patronage was crucial to advancement, and most Roman sources laid great stress on it. All patronage systems were ultimately linked to a kingdom's ruler as chief patron. The patron–client relationship had existed in most societies, but Roman culture laid immense stress on it, and most people accepted it.[12] Augustine would also have been heavily dependent on the patronage of the Frankish bishops, Queen Brunhild and her two grandchildren, no doubt some members of the wealthy landed aristocracy and, most of all, on Queen Bertha and Aethelberht of Kent. Pope Gregory's lack of attention to this at the beginning of the mission cost Augustine dearly in terms of lost time, extending his journey through the territories of Francia into the harshest part of winter.

Wealth

Wealth was hugely important, except perhaps for a few high-minded bishops, although by this period, nearly all the bishops were also members of the aristocracy; and if they weren't at the time of their consecration, then becoming a bishop would make them so. Wealth and power were overwhelmingly based on the land – and the Church was a major landowner.[13] One important exception to the attitude to wealth in the late Roman period was the Church's involvement in charity to the poor, which had been a mainstay of Christian community activity from the beginning (Acts 2.4). Not least, care of the poor – through alms, hospitals and education – also provided a justification for the Church's growing wealth, one that was different from the personal accumulation that characterized most of the aristocracy and the senatorial class.

The City

Political society still focused on the cities; they were the centre of almost all political activity, and the places where Christians were usually numerically dominant. Being a city councillor was the height of local ambition, but city government became more informal, based on the local rich as a collective group, but without specific institutions. Senators who also lived locally, the civic bishop and the wealthiest councillors made up this ad-hoc elite group of 'leading men'. They patronized city churches, made decisions about building repairs and festivals and if necessary organized local defence. Private armies raised by such leading men also defended some of the cities.

Peasants

The population of the late Empire consisted overwhelmingly of the peasantry, families of cultivators who worked their own land or rented land and lived off the food they themselves produced. The peasants surrendered their surpluses in rents to landlords, and in taxes to the State. By now both free and unfree peasants lived their lives in similar ways. 'Slaves' in this period refers to unfree domestic servants, who were fed and maintained by their masters as plantation labourers. The cathedral church was often, by 500, the largest landowner and therefore a major patron. It was ecclesiastical wealth and local status that led the episcopate to become part of the elite structures in fifth-century Francia; and by 550 it was normal practice everywhere.[14] The traditional hierarchy of the Roman world had effectively absorbed the new power structures of Christianity.

Bishops

The office of bishop in Gaul had become a standard part of a secular career progression for city notables, just as pagan priesthood had been two centuries earlier. A secular career at a royal court was becoming another route by the late sixth century, and Gregory rebuked the French Church for the practice of simony (the purchase of an office).[15] There were two levels of bishops – metropolitans (archbishops) at an intermediate level beneath the pope or eastern patriarch overseeing and consecrating the bishops of each province. As the Church was more stable over time as a political institution than most of the secular powers, the political power of bishops steadily increased.

The early medieval mind was profoundly different from the present-day, and religion, both belief and right practice, was serious business. For Christian Rome, as for the Franks since Clovis I, this was a world that believed in miracles and that God was active in his creation. In a world that could see battle as a judgement of God, death itself carried certain connotations. A battle could be seen as a judicial ordeal, in which the winner and loser demonstrated God's approval or disapproval. A king could not possibly hope to win a battle without the Almighty's approval. The Merovingian kings carried Saint Martin's cloak with them to battle for this reason.

The bishops' prayers before and absolution of the troops from guilt after battle made the same point. In these ways, rulers attempted to load the odds in their favour and increase their chances of victory.[16] The late Roman mindset also handed a privileged place to the bishops in their relationship with the king and in their influence in state affairs other than war. The kings, in turn, had the power to depose and appoint new bishops, so the relationship in terms of hierarchy was finely balanced.

Ascetics

Ascetics, however, broke all late Roman social rules: few were aristocratic, few were educated, but people sought their advice persistently, and some were revered as saints. Relics of saints began to be associated with major churches as early as the fourth century, and miracles were associated with them, as the murder of Archbishop Thomas à Becket in Saint Augustine's cathedral in Canterbury on 27 December 1170 would also come to illustrate. Veneration of the relics of saints and martyrs fuelled a growing pilgrimage phenomenon that involved travelling great distances and was initially centred on Jerusalem as the location of the death, resurrection and ascension of Jesus, with relics of the True Cross and the Holy Blood. This changed dramatically with the fall of Jerusalem to the followers of Muhammad in 636. Rome, as possessor of the relics of the two great apostles of the Early Church, Saint Peter and Saint Paul, took up the mantle and became the major pilgrimage destination in Christendom by the late seventh century.

Superstition

Superstitions of one form or another were universally held by all sections of the population. Religious practices and sacrifices were overwhelmingly concerned with winning the favour of the gods, achieving good fortune, ensuring the fertility of women, livestock and crops and every other aspect of everyday living. Performing signs and wonders was still important for both pagans and Christians alike. However, Christianity placed more public emphasis than pagans on human interventions in supernatural affairs – through prayer, fasting, intercession – particularly if they held formal church authority as bishops or clergy or if they themselves were particularly holy, as many ascetics were. Miracles were essential both to the Church as evidence for sainthood and individually also for holy men and ascetics in winning a hearing and attracting a following.

Women

Constraints on women increased in this period, although those who pursued a monastic life were marginally better placed. Legally, women lived under the control of men. Husbands still controlled a couple's property; fathers retained some authority over their children through *patria potestas* (fatherly power).[17] The wives of monarchs are a significant exception. In this period, both Brunhild of Austrasia and Fredegund of Neustria possessed considerable wealth on their own account, some from their dowries, others from gifts and from taxes raised in the cities given to them.

Education

By Late Antiquity, classical education based on Latin grammar, rhetoric and literature was rapidly disappearing. Gregory of Tours bemoaned the absence of great schools that produced grammarians. It is perhaps in this sense that some have spoken of the lights going out all over Europe, expressing the view that the monasteries alone carried the light of civilization through the Dark Ages. With the decline of the grammar schools the skills of writing and the teaching of grammar shifted almost completely to the monasteries. Yet, the Merovingians had court tutors, who taught the royals language and writing skills, poetry and law during the sixth century and beyond, and a basic Latin grammar education does not seem to have disappeared from Rome in this period, nor in Constantinople or Ravenna.

Hierarchy

Nearly all writers of the period took social hierarchy for granted, as well as a belief in the innate moral virtue of their own aristocratic social stratum. The universal assumption that men were intrinsically superior to women was a given in a masculine culture. Servility to social superiors and the coercion of social inferiors were normal practice. People in this period are different from us, but are still extremely interesting.[18] Only a few people from this period would one want to meet with any anticipation of pleasure – one of them is Gregory the Great, who for the historian Bede is the central character of the Augustinian mission to England.

Notes

1 Robin Cormack and Maria Vassilaki, *Byzantium 330–1453*, London: Royal Academy of Arts, 2008, p. 27.

2 L. K. Little, *Plague and the End of Antiquity: The Pandemic of 541–750*, New York: Cambridge University Press, 2007, p. 3.

3 Matthew Sturgis, *When in Rome: 2000 Years of Roman Sightseeing*, London: Frances Lincoln Limited (Kindle book), 2011, p. 938.

4 John Julius Norwich, *The Popes: A History*, London: Chatto & Windus, 2011, pp. 38–42.

5 Sturgis, *When in Rome*, p. 1377.

6 Chris Wickham, *The Inheritance of Rome: A History of Europe from 400 to 1000*, London: Penguin Books, 2010, p. 21.

7 Ian Wood, *The Merovingian Kingdoms, 450–751*, London and New York: Longman, 1994, p. 69.

8 Robert Knapp, *Invisible Romans*, London: Profile Books (iBook), 2011, pp. 200ff.

9 Rowan Williams, 'Relations between the Church and state today: What is the role of the Christian citizen?', 2011, at www.archbishopofcanterbury.org/articles.php/2009/relations-between-the-church-and-state-today-what-is-the-role-of-the-christian-citizen.

10 Wickham, *Inheritance of Rome*, Chs. 2–3.

11 Gregory the Great, Book VI, Letter 7 to the Presbyter Candidus. The letters of Pope Gregory can be found at the New Advent website, http://www.newadvent.org/fathers/3602.htm. Future references will give the Book and Letter numbers only.

12 Wickham, *Inheritance of Rome*, p. 22.

13 Wickham, *Inheritance of Rome*, p. 16.

14 Wickham, *Inheritance of Rome*, Ch. 2.

15 Gregory the Great, *Book VI*, Letter 7 to the Presbyter Candidus.

16 Guy Halsall, *Warfare and Society in the Barbarian West, 450–900*, London: Routledge, 2003, p. 6.

17 Halsall, *Warfare*, p. 97.

18 Wickham, *Inheritance of Rome*, p. 552.

2

Gregory the Great and Saint Andrew's Monastery in Rome

After a year as Prefect of Rome Gregory withdrew from public life and in 575 established a monastery on his estate on the Caelian Hill, one of the Seven Hills of Rome. Gregory established a further six communities in Sicily on his family estates. From the first century, Christian communities around the Mediterranean gathered in large houses and villas for worship and hospitality. The conversion of spacious domestic buildings, such as large town houses and estate villas, to oratories for personal, family or monastic use was well established by the sixth century.[1] A similar pattern is discernible in Roman Britain from the mid-fourth century.

Saint Andrew's Monastery in Rome

Gregory's seven monasteries, all dedicated to Saint Andrew, may have been unusual in that they were not attached to a major basilica, as were Saint Peter's and Saint Paul's which lay outside the city walls. Saint Andrew's Rome, renamed *Santi Andrea e Gregorio Magno a Celio* after Gregory's death, was not the first such family-based religious community in Rome, even within his own family. Three of Gregory's aunts had adopted the religious life, one of them according to Gregory attaining to the heights of holiness by her prayer, the dignity of her living and her outstanding self-denial.[2] Local tradition at Saint Gregory's Monastery recalls that his mother had converted her home into a religious community well before Gregory. In pursuit of *conversatio morum* (conversion from a life in the world to a life in a monastic community), her household had followed her.

Gregory's *domus* in Rome commanded a strategic location within the city. In former times, it would have comprised quarters for slaves, various outbuildings, stables and extensive gardens near the foot of the hill. The estate was bounded on the north by a narrow street, the Clevis Scauri,[3] which crosses the Caelian Hill from east to west. It joined a broader avenue to the west, the present day Via di San Gregorio leading to the Colosseum. The town house on the estate overlooked the Palatine Hill further to the west. For most of Gregory's life the entire Palatine complex, from the Roman Forum to the Circus Maximus, lay deserted in a state of ruin. Owing to the severe shortages in Rome, Saint Andrew's Monastery would have grown much of its own food to feed both its monks and lay brothers, but also the growing number of visitors and pilgrims to Rome.

Gregory's Role at Saint Andrew's

Gregory was pater familias of the family estates by 575, following the death of his father Gordianus. The newly formed monastery would have included his entire household. In the Roman world of the sixth century the role of the head of a family had changed little since the founding of Rome. To be a member of a Roman family was to be under the religious, financial and disciplinary power of the father until death. From earliest times monasteries have drawn on the support and labour of lay associates comprising both families and unmarried members. Saint Andrew's gave the estate's slaves – household staff, labourers, gardeners, carpenters, potters, builders, stable hands and others – more freedom, as a religious community of monks and lay members, than they would have formerly enjoyed as slaves on the estate. These skills would be vital for Augustine's mission to Kent, where the agricultural and horticultural practices were far less developed than in Rome.

Although Gregory held the traditional role of pater familias, there is no evidence that he was also abbot of his own monastery. This fell to Valentio, who served as abbot of a substantially lay community comprising anchorites and coenobites (solitaries or hermits, as well as those living in community). Each member lived according to an individual rule of life agreed with the abbot and shared a common daily pattern of life and worship. Scribes, educators, craftsmen and manuscript illuminators would also be drawn to the monastery over the next 20 years, and these skills would later provide Augustine with the essential elements for establishing a monastic school for young, aristocratic Anglo-Saxons in Canterbury.

Constantinople

Despite his commitment to the monastic life, Gregory was too valuable to the city to be left in retirement, and in 578 Pope Benedict I appointed him as one of the seven Deacons (Regionarii) of Rome. A year later, Pope Pelagius II sent Gregory as ambassador to the imperial court in Constantinople. Gregory took with him a number of monks from Saint Andrew's Monastery, including the abbot Maximian, who was to succeed Valentio as abbot. Together they constituted an outpost of Saint Andrew's, a monastic community in the Imperial City. Recalled to Rome from Constantinople after nine years, Gregory returned to Saint Andrew's in 587, devoting himself to reading, writing, contemplation and the exposition of the Scriptures. He considered this the happiest period of his life. His hagiography of Benedict may have been written during this time. Benedict's monks had fled to Rome after the Lombard destruction of Monte Cassino in 585. They found refuge initially near the Lateran Palace, making Benedict's Rule and the stories of his life readily accessible to Gregory, who was Benedict's only biographer. However, there is nothing to suggest that Saint Andrew's adopted the Benedictine Rule during Gregory's lifetime, and Augustine did not introduce it at Canterbury.

Gregory as Bishop of Rome

On 28 December 589, 14 years after founding Saint Andrew's Monastery, Gregory finalized the handing over of the estate to the community. Already a Papal Deacon, and within a few months of his election as Bishop of Rome, Gregory issued a charter granting the land and properties to the monastery. This freed Gregory from a major burden of secular care and resolved a long-standing tension over property ownership and management felt by many of his aristocratic contemporaries. In return, this arrangement offered him a contemplative life within a supportive monastic community. However, events took a dramatically different course.

When Pelagius II unexpectedly died of the plague in February 590, Gregory was again called back to public ministry, on this occasion as Bishop of Rome. His earlier labours in the service of the Holy See made him the obvious if reluctant successor to Pelagius.[4] Gregory's association with Saint Andrew's appears to have remained close during his pontificate; he selected one of its members to mount an expedition to England and committed monks and lay brothers to the mission.

There has been an unbroken community on the present site of Saint Gregory's Monastery since 575.[5] Although not Benedictine from the outset, the community adopted the Rule of Saint Benedict somewhere between 610 and 655. In this period, there were several monastic Rules that an abbot could draw from, and it was not until 610 that a Synod of Italian bishops was held in Rome to draw up regulations concerning monastic life and harmony.[6]

Saint Andrew's Monastery – Preparation for Mission

Behind the present imposing façade of Saint Gregory's Monastery, visitors and pilgrims enter an atrium suggestive of the original town house. Unexcavated remains lie beneath the present entrance, chapel and cloisters. The smaller Chapel of Saint Gregory, at the end of the south aisle of the present church, is adjacent to a room believed to incorporate the remains of Gregory's anchorite cell within its fabric.

Gregory's monastery remained a working estate after conversion to a monastic community. Rome's frequent food shortages made it vital that the community be self-sufficient in staples of fruit, vegetables, milk and cheese. Almsgiving to the poor including meals would have been a daily occurrence. A chapel in the grounds has an antique stone table at which Gregory is said to have hosted the poor who came to the monastery. Saint Andrew's central location in the city would guarantee a constant stream of guests, keeping Gregory and the community in touch with events elsewhere, including fresh currents of thinking and scholarship from communities all over the Christian world. Gregory's election and consecration as Bishop of Rome in 590 drew many of his supporters to the city and to Saint Andrew's from all over the Western and Eastern Church, including representatives from Tours. When Gregory came to mount a mission to England, he would have taken for granted that his missionaries would receive hospitality, shelter and support on their journey through Francia.

The timing of events was crucial to Saint Andrew's readiness in launching the mission. Developments over the 20 years before 596 had prepared Saint Andrew's for its involvement in mission to the Anglo-Saxon world. A typical monastery in this period comprised 25 monks and many more lay brothers. Together they possessed a breadth of specialization in skills that would be vital for a long-term mission – building and carpentry skills, writing and parchment-making, musical and liturgical skills, preaching ability and competence in biblical studies. As Augustine would discover in Canterbury, the Anglo-Saxons could neither read nor write, and the ability to record the deeds of kings for posterity would be a small but significant monopoly in the hands of the Church.

Gregory's Leadership as Bishop of Rome

Gregory's leadership abilities were considerable. He was born into one of the foremost senatorial families in Rome, possessing extensive properties in and around the capital as well as in Sicily. The family had a long association with the Roman Church; Felix III (pope 483–92) was Gregory's great-great-grandfather. Gregory's father Gordianus had been a senior official of the Roman Church, and his mother and three of his aunts also entered the religious life.

Gregory, the first monk to become Bishop of Rome, granted important privileges to his monks and chose them for his immediate circle. Edward Gibbon, who was no friend of the Church and frequently critical in his judgement, felt moved to write: 'The pontificate of Gregory the Great, which lasted thirteen years, six months, and ten days, is one of the most edifying periods of the history of the church.'[7]

Although frequently stricken with illness during his pontificate, Gregory's enormous energy is apparent in his surviving correspondence, biblical commentaries and other writings. His Rule of Pastoral Care, written in the early months of his pontificate, laid the groundwork for the kind of leadership he was to exercise over the next 13 years. Gregory was highly educated in the traditional disciplines of Roman culture, and his contemporary Gregory of Tours considered that in grammar, rhetoric and dialectic he was second to none in Rome.[8] His commentary on Job indicates the scope of his biblical exegesis. Although by the late sixth century there was no longer a major institution of religious learning to be found in Rome, Gregory is reckoned to have belonged to the best educated elite. Gregory was steeped in the works of both the bishop–theologian Augustine of Hippo and the writings of the monastic author John Cassian of Marseille.

The ontological question that had occupied Augustine of Hippo – *Who is a Christian?* – had moved on in the intervening two centuries so that the wisdom issue now most occupying Gregory's thinking was, *How shall we live?* This was a concern he shared with Benedict whose Rule (written 50 or so years before Gregory's *Regula Pastoralis* for bishops) furnished a monastic response to the social crises of the time. Gregory's Pastoral Rule can be regarded as a secular counterpart to Benedict's monastic rule.

Gregory believed that although secular learning had value, it provided no armour for spiritual warfare. Secular learning was subordinate to scriptural learning and a means of deepening it, but only to the extent that this promoted scriptural understanding. He wrote a letter to Desiderius, Metropolitan of Vienne in Burgundy, expressing his concern for the bishop over this issue. Gregory stood squarely in the tradition of Augustine and the statesman–monk Cassiodorus (d. 585), but with the radical difference that he believed the secular world could have little significance against the backdrop of the endtime drama that was – in his view – about to be played out.

The chief concern in Gregory's exposition of the Scriptures (from his discourses on the Book of Job onwards) was what the Scriptures had to say about the Christian moral life. Reading the Scriptures was a moral exercise that deepened both faith and love. The Bible is the doorway, but through Christ alone we have access to salvation. Conversion is the end result of understanding the Scriptures, and to understand the Scriptures is to be renewed through their power. Gregory accepted the authority of Scripture and expected miracles as the sign of any true saint, as his biography of Benedict shows. Like Benedict, he used biblical texts to support a particular position already held.

Gregory was more interested in finding spiritual truth from an interpretation of the text than in expounding its contextual meaning. His understanding of the significance of preaching was wholly consistent with Paul's Letter to the Romans 10.14: 'But how are they to call on one in whom they have not believed? And how are they to believe in one of whom they have never heard? And how are they to hear without someone to proclaim him?' 'Hearing the Word', so central to monastic 'obedient listening', was no less crucial for the work of mission, and the mission to England would rely heavily upon those who could preach Good News to the Anglo-Saxon peoples in their native tongue.

Much of Gregory's writings concerning leadership and the Church were directed towards reintroducing humble, Christ-like service. In his view, ministry and the exercise of authority were works of love, and the exercise of authority must be carried out with humility, so that those ruled should develop free rather than coerced humility. Crucially for Gregory the bishop was the servant of the servants of Christ's community. His role was to be productive (*prodesse*) rather than pre-eminent (*praesse*). This was the keynote of his papacy.

Gregory's Motives for Mission

Three years before launching the English mission, Gregory anguished over the deteriorating situation in Rome: 'Where now is the Senate? Where the people? . . . The Senate is gone, the people perish; pain and fear grow daily for the few who are left; a deserted Rome is burning . . . we see buildings destroyed, ruins daily multiplied.'[9]

Unlike the North African bishop and theologian Augustine, Gregory held out no hope of this world's regeneration – it was doomed. He lived in constant eschatological anticipation of the Last Days, and his perception of current events gave him little reason to believe otherwise. Mission in these end times was a Gospel imperative that Gregory intended to honour, particularly in his desire to convert the pagan lands to the northwest. A risky venture such as this, into a remote territory beyond the protection of Roman legions and at a time when Italy itself had substantially lost its own territorial integrity to invading Germanic tribes, was an extraordinary act of courage and hope for his time.

A combination of factors seems more probable than one single motive for the launch of the English mission in 596. Gregory was looking for an opportunity to expand the Roman Church in the face of increasing conflict with the Eastern Church encircling the Mediterranean region. The Eastern Patriarch in Constantinople had appropriated to himself the title *Pontifex Maximus* and this had strained his relationship with Gregory. There was also a desire to renew and strengthen bonds with the Frankish Church after a long period of comparative neglect and to enlist the backing of powerful Frankish rulers such as Queen Brunhild. And not least there existed an apostolic impulse to take the gospel to the ends of the earth and if possible to hasten in these seemingly Last Days the coming of the Kingdom.

The most crucial element is that the *Angli* became the focus of Gregory's apostolic mission once he had received information that the English people were placed in a corner of the world and still faithless, worshipping sticks and stones, and that they wished to be converted. A further attraction for Gregory was that the Anglo-Saxons were 'true' heathens: they were not infected by the Arian controversy that had convulsed the Mediterranean world and many of the Germanic tribes in particular.[10] This included the Lombards who occupied much of Italy. The Merovingian Franks were a striking exception.

The Venerable Bede, eighth-century historian of the English people and monk at Jarrow in Northumberland, possessed first-hand knowledge of the unremitting savagery perpetrated by his own Anglo-Saxon race in the late seventh and early eighth centuries. He offered his own understanding of the apostolic motivation behind Gregory's mission, as one of its beneficiaries.'Gregory, prompted by divine inspiration, sent a servant of God named of God to the English race.'[11] Bede goes on to interpret Gregory's view of the heathen condition of the English: 'He converted our nation, that is, the nation of the English, from the power of Satan to the faith of Christ . . . our nation hitherto enslaved to idols he made into a church.'[12]

Gregory knew very little about the state of England or the indigenous British Church, now largely confined to Wales, Cumbria and the West Country (Somerset, Devon and Cornwall). Crucial as England was to be for the future of Catholicism in the West, Gregory had only a limited amount of time or energy to give to the Augustinian mission, and very little of his surviving correspondence in his Papal *Regesta* is devoted to it.

The mission to England was probably not something that stemmed from a long-cherished papal plan to reconvert a former

Roman province. Whatever secondary benefits might accrue from such a mission, Gregory's principal impulse appears to be a pastoral response to a request from a source in Kent to send a mission for the conversion of the Anglo-Saxons. Gregory's concern was for saving souls, not for restoring lost imperial provinces. He was, however, clearly concerned to extend the influence of the Church of Rome.

Choosing a monk who had spent most of his adult life in a monastic community to lead a mission to the English, in preference to one of the pope's secular clergy, might at first seem unusual. After all, preaching to believers and non-believers was the solemn duty laid upon the clergy, and in Gregory's understanding, mission and the pastoral ministry formed an indissoluble unity. However, preaching to his bishops in the Lateran Basilica, Gregory had said: 'Behold, the world is full of priests, and yet workmen in the Lord's harvest are hard to find because although we have taken the priestly office, we do not fulfil its obligations.'[13]

The Frankish bishops who were closest to England had failed to honour their obligations. The charge to preach the Good News to the heathen at the ends of the earth must now fall to the monks, who were members of a fast-growing lay movement, with only a loose association with diocesan authority and structures, or it would not be achieved at all.

It is significant that, in making this choice, Gregory brought the monastery (or *mynster* in Anglo-Saxon) to the forefront as the principal instrument of mission in England for the next three centuries. The idea for the mission to England may well not have been original to Gregory, but the central role of the monastery in mission certainly was. His leadership undoubtedly ranks in the highest order of any age.

Augustine's Biography to 596

In striking contrast to how much we know about Gregory, little if anything is known of Augustine before 596. One tradition claims that Augustine was a Sicilian by birth, and at his confirmation took his name from Augustine of Hippo; another that, physically, he stood head and shoulders above the other members of his company.[14] He is also said to have entered a seminary in Sicily, possibly becoming a pupil of Felix, Bishop of Messina, who was styled a *consodolis* (companion) of Augustine.[15] Or Augustine might simply have come from Rome. Whatever the case, he was a trusted member of the community when Gregory commissioned him to lead the mission to England.

The process of Augustine's inner formation – his spiritual life, character and discipleship as a monk – was common to most communities. Spiritual formation combined the disciplines of daily prayer, the *opus dei* (seven or eight daily offices of corporate chapel worship), with the development of character through a process of obedient 'listening' – to the abbot, the community Rule and the Scriptures – and through private study, manual labour and administrative work. Gregory believed that the unskilled should not assume pastoral authority: 'No one presumes to teach an art till he has first, with intent meditation, learnt it. What rashness is it, then, for the unskilful to assume pastoral authority, since the government of souls is the art of arts?'[16]

As the person chosen to lead the English mission, Augustine had clearly met Gregory's criteria for skills in pastoral leadership as well as spiritual maturity. In a subsequent letter to Aethelberht, the Kentish king, Gregory would praise Augustine as one who was brought up under a monastic Rule, filled with the knowledge of the Holy Scriptures and endowed with good works through the grace of God.[17]

Augustine's competence in spiritual and pastoral leadership was apparently matched by his organizing abilities. When Gregory entrusted the mission to Augustine, he was far from an unknown quantity in terms of his competence in both practical and spiritual matters. Augustine would have been known to Gregory both as a fellow brother in Saint Andrew's Monastery and, from 590, as one of the many officials of the papal chancery responsible for church property in Rome. Augustine's efficient administration of the lay stewards of the 'villas of endowment' (i.e. church property) had evidently earned him the position of sub-prior in Gregory's monastery, a monastic position that was attained only after years of experience. Overseeing the day-to-day affairs of the monastery and supervising the lay stewards of the villas of endowment would have provided ample evidence of Augustine's competence, stability and leadership in a variety of situations.

The year 596 had intimately involved St Andrew's monastery in preparations for the expedition to England. In effect, Augustine was given responsibility for a travelling monastery. The conception of the mission was an act of remarkable originality: the Roman Church had not sent a group of monks to preach to a heathen people before, although individuals had conducted missions, as Patrick had in Ireland, Ninian in Scotland and Columbanus in Francia and Italy. This monastic enterprise was both the forerunner and blueprint of the way that Christianity would expand in both the south and the north of England, as Aidan's seventh-century mission to Northumbria would prove.

In perhaps May or June 596 Augustine and his group of monks and lay brothers, carrying a silver processional cross and a painted icon of Christ in their baggage, left behind a Rome beset by problems on every side. Neither Bede's nor Gregory's letters indicate how many accompanied Augustine, only that the combined party of monks and priests that finally landed on the shores of Kent numbered about forty people.[18] As emissaries of the pope, their mission was urgent; there was much unfinished business, as the conversion of the Anglo-Saxons was to show, and in these apocalyptic days, with barbarians again approaching the gates of Rome, there was little time to lose.

Who Requested a Mission to the Anglo-Saxon People?

Gregory believed that the English themselves eagerly desired the mission. In a letter to two Frankish rulers delivered by Augustine during his journey through Francia, Gregory wrote:

> And thus it has reached us that the English nation, by the compassion of God, eagerly desires to be converted to the Christian faith, but that neighbouring [Frankish] bishops neglect it and refrain from kindling by their exhortation the desires of the English . . . On this account, therefore, we have arranged to send thither Augustine, the servant of God . . .[19]

There is no indication as to who these eager supplicants were on behalf of 'the English nation'. The only credible source of a request for assistance lies within the Kentish royal court itself, particularly from its most senior Frankish Christian member Queen Bertha and King Aethelberht. Gregory indicates that the English nation had already made a request to the Frankish Church, but that no support had been forthcoming. The Frankish bishops, according to Pope Gregory, showed no inclination to provide a mission to the English. Effectively abandoned by her own Church, Bertha would have acutely felt the absence of Frankish support.

Before Augustine's arrival in Francia, it seems unlikely that Gregory had a source of information about the circumstances of Aethelberht's royal court that was independent of Queen Bertha. A view expressed by the Prior of Saint Gregory's Monastery in Rome (in 2004), Dom Innocenzo Gargano, is that Gregory was a pragmatist rather than a visionary; he would not have initiated such a mission had the request not come from the highest level, that is, from Queen Bertha herself.[20]

From a purely logistical perspective, it seems inconceivable that a large missionary party from Rome, travelling under difficult circumstances through divided and bitterly opposing Frankish kingdoms, could land unannounced on the Kent coast with a substantial party of people who possessed no visible means of support and expect to be welcomed (let alone materially supported), unless they had already received such an assurance from the queen – and behind her, the active support of the king.

Context is important in assessing the various alternatives. Gregory, as a Roman aristocrat who viewed the world in hierarchical terms, would not have taken his cue for a mission from the testimony of two young slaves. They could not in any sense be said to speak for 'the English nation', as Pope Gregory states in his letter to the young kings, Theuderic and Theudebert. On the contrary, with an almost universal view of hierarchical power and authority held throughout this period, the only person Gregory would expect to speak for 'the nation' would be its ruler.

Ostia, Port of Rome

Augustine and his companions left Rome in May or June 596. They undoubtedly carried in their baggage tools, manuscripts and equipment needed for a mission to a far country. However, what they did not have with them were letters of introduction or commendation from Pope Gregory to the noblemen, bishops and kings they would meet on their journey though Francia. This was a significant omission on Gregory's part, one that would cost them dearly by extending their journey into winter and delaying their arrival in Canterbury by several long months.

The journey from Rome would take Augustine downstream on the River Tiber to the port of Ostia. As the Germanic Lombard tribes controlled much of the area around the city of Rome, a journey through northern Italy was not feasible. Even travelling to Ostia the relatively short distance by road would be hazardous.

Travelling to the coastal port on a three day journey would begin at the docks on the western edge of the Aventine district, on a merchant ship returning from Rome. The best time of year for sailing was reckoned to be from the beginning of March to the middle of September, as unpredictable trade winds threatened for the rest of the year. Vessels typically sailed into Ostia's harbour in the afternoon and sailed out in the morning, a practice due entirely to the regularity of the breeze blowing from the sea in the afternoon and from the land in the morning.

By the end of the sixth century Ostia's status as the Port of Rome was in terminal decline. The nearby harbour complex of Portus had completely overshadowed Ostia as a port since the early fourth century, and Ostia became a summer residence for Roman aristocracy. However, by 537 the picture had again changed dramatically; Portus was seized by the Goths under Vitigis and rapidly declined as Rome's major port. From this period on, only smaller ships – 150 tons or less – could manage the river journey to Rome. Larger vessels unloaded their cargo off the coast at Ostia, transferring their loads to smaller vessels. It was a difficult operation to unload cargo safely from ships anchored offshore, resulting in a diminished supply of food destined for Rome and much reduced shipping traffic on the Tiber.

The sight of large cargo ships unable to land at Portus or Ostia would be a poignant reminder to Augustine of an ancient biblical warning concerning Rome:

> The merchants of the earth weep and mourn for her, since no one buys their cargo any more, cargo of gold, silver, jewels and pearls, fine linen, purple, silk and scarlet, all kinds of scented wood, all articles of ivory, all articles of costly wood, bronze, iron, and marble, cinnamon, spice, incense, myrrh, frankincense, wine, olive oil, choice flour and wheat, cattle and sheep, horses and chariots, slaves – and human lives. (Revelation 18.11)

Ostia's population had suffered a major decline in the years before 596. At the end of the fifth century, Ostia's aqueduct had ceased functioning, restricting the supply of clean water to the city. By the last decades of the sixth century the city's residents lived among abandoned and decaying buildings. The former theatre had been turned into a small fortress. From this point, the recorded history of Ostia becomes a blank. The port was abandoned after Lombard attempts to control the coast at some time after 590, but Ostia still functioned as a town. Augustine's mission was launched by June 596. Had Gregory delayed much longer, within a matter of months it might have been impossible for a party to leave Rome at all.

If the missionary party set sail on or near 29 June 596, the Feast Day of Saint Peter and Saint Paul, Augustine would have had a specific reason to dedicate his own monastic outpost built outside the walls of the city of Canterbury to these two saints. Dedications of monasteries to the apostles Peter and Paul were common throughout the monastic world in the absence of a shrine dedicated to a local saint.

Ostia also possessed one characteristic that was to prove highly relevant to Augustine's mission to Anglo-Saxon England: archaeological evidence shows that, although Christianity had been the official religion of the Roman State for almost two centuries, Ostia tolerated at least a dozen pagan cults that were still practised alongside Christian worship by the end of the sixth century. Global trade was the business of the port of Ostia, and the local attitude to religious pluralism was evidently laissez-faire. As events in England would prove, some syncretism in religious belief and practice would need to be tolerated by the Church for some considerable time.

The Sea Route

David Abulafia describes typical sailing conditions during this period: 'Everything and everyone on board were tightly packed together, and travellers slept under the stars, using their possessions as pillow and mattress.'[21] Merchants loaded their goods on board the day before departure and stayed with them to prevent theft or breakages during the journey. The development of decking over the hold and the luxury of a cabin fore and aft would not arise until the eleventh century. Ships carrying grain, wine and oil to Rome might typically return home without a cargo, the necessary ballast provided by Roman bricks stacked in the hold. Even at the height of the Empire's grain trade, smaller ships significantly outnumbered large grain carriers. A displacement of 50 tons may have been typical and the ability to carry more than 70 people unusual.

Augustine's sea journey was more than 315 miles from Ostia to the island of Saint-Honorat on the Frankish Côte d'Azur. Under favourable circumstances, vessels sailing from the mouth of the Tiber could reach Alexandria and the Nile in 11 days; the Straits of Gibraltar in seven; the Straits of Messina and even the Albanian coast in five; the coast of Barcelona in four and the coast of Africa in less than two. Under ideal conditions, Augustine's journey to the Gulf of Marseille would take at least three days.

From the outset, timing would prove crucial in the course of the mission. With the fluctuating fortunes of Rome's naval conflict against raiders from the sea and the frequent sacking and siege of Ostia during the course of these battles, a decision to sail to Provence from the port of Ostia would be as much a matter of providence as good judgement.

Notes

1 John Percival, *The Roman Villa*, London: Pitman Press, 1976, p. 183.
2 R. A. Markus, *Gregory the Great and His World*, Cambridge: Cambridge University Press, 1997, p. 8.
3 Lit. 'climb of Scaurus', named after an Etruscan soldier who came to the aid of Rome in defence of the city.
4 Markus, *Gregory*, pp. 8–14.
5 The monastery church is dedicated to Santi Andrea e Gregorio Magno a Celio. In 1629–33. Scipione Cardinal Cafarelli Borghese commissioned its renovation to a design by Giovanni Battista Soria. The monastery is home to Camaldolese monks, Benedictines distinguished by wearing a white habit.
6 Bede, *Ecclesiastical History* II.4.
7 Edward Gibbon, *The Decline and Fall of the Roman Empire*, Vol. IV, London: Everyman's Library, 1994, p. 533.
8 Markus, *Gregory*, p. 34.
9 Markus, *Gregory*, p. 52.
10 Henry Mayr-Harting, *The Coming of Christianity to Anglo-Saxon England*, London: B. T. Batsford, 1972, p. 60.
11 Bede, *Ecclesiastical History* I.26.
12 Bede, *Ecclesiastical History* II.1.
13 Markus, *Gregory*, p. 80.
14 H. F. Bing, 'St. Augustine of Canterbury and the Saxon Church', *Archaeologia Cantiana* 62 (1949), p. 111.
15 David Hugh Farmer, *Oxford Dictionary of Saints*, Oxford: Clarendon Press, 1978, p. 30.

16 Gregory the Great, *The Book of Pastoral Rule*, Medieval
   Source Book, www.fordham.edu/halsall/source/590greg1-pas
   toralrule2.html, Part 1 Ch. 1.
17 Bede, *Ecclesiastical History* I.32.
18 Bede, *Ecclesiastical History* I.25.
19 Gregory the Great, Book IV, Letter 58 to Theuderic and
   Theudebert.
20 Comments in a private conversation with the Prior at Saint
   Gregory's Monastery in Rome, 3 June 2004.
21 David Abulafia, *The Great Sea: A Human History of the Mediterranean*, London: Allen Lane (Penguin) (iBook), 2011, p. 316.

3

First Landing in Provence

Lérins Abbey

Augustine probably landed at the port of Villefranche on the Côte d'Azur. The distance from Villefranche to Cannes over the ancient Roman *Via Aurelia* is about 25 miles (40 km), followed by a ferry crossing of a little less than four miles to the landing place at Saint-Honorat. Fifteen minutes' walk from the landing on the northern shore would bring the missionaries to the monastery on the south side of the island.

Whether or not Abbot Stephen of Lérins had expected Augustine's arrival, hospitality for the monks would, as a matter of course, be forthcoming. Saint-Honorat may seem somewhat remote today, but like many monasteries of the sixth and later centuries, it was able to use the sea as an essential highway to other monastic communities throughout the Mediterranean, providing mutual support, exchanging documents and offering hospitality to monks, pilgrims and travellers.

The island was named after its founder Honoratus (c. 350–429) in about 410. Lérins was the Gallo-Roman Church's second monastic community, following after Saint Martin's Monastery near Tours some 40 years earlier. Honoratus was the leading member of a monastic movement drawn largely from Gallo-Roman aristocracy. Lérins had achieved widespread fame for its role in the newly emerging intellectual world as the direct influence of Rome declined.[1] Augustine would meet with bishops formed in this mould during his journey through Francia.

The missionaries were apparently well received by Abbot Stephen, the first in Francia to welcome Augustine and his companions on their expedition to England. However, it is clear from the letter Gregory wrote to accompany Augustine on his second visit to Lérins that all was not well in the monastery. Stephen himself was no longer abbot by 600, when Gregory wrote to Corbon, the abbot's successor.

The *Via Aurelia* to Aquae Sextiae

Much of Julius Caesar's route to reach Britannia in the first century BC would become familiar to Augustine some six centuries later on his own journey through Francia. The only feasible route by road from Cannes to Aquae Sextiae (Aix-en-Provence) at the end of the sixth century was on the *Via Aurelia,* a distance of about 100 miles. Augustine's first aim was to meet with Bishop Protasius, travelling west along the coastal route of the *Aurelia,* then north to Aix. Also on his agenda was a meeting with the patrician magnate Arigius, civil governor of Provence, and a long-standing correspondent with Gregory.[2]

In the summer of 596, Augustine would have found the *Via Aurelia* jostling with travellers' wagons and carts, messengers on horseback and warriors attached to the households of local aristocratic families. Augustine, travelling with a party of companions, wagons and mules carrying baggage that comprised tools, books and manuscripts for study and worship and tents for their overnight stops, would not make rapid headway. The going could be slow on crowded roads. In summer months, travellers would be up and on the road by 6am, stopping by mid-afternoon to make camp if there was no other lodging, forage for firewood, cook a meal, care for the mules, find water and make repairs. In earlier times, the Roman army could cover ten miles in three and a half hours. For Augustine and other travellers it was not unusual to travel only six miles a day, and on a very good day those travelling light might cover 13–17 miles.

Francia at the End of the Sixth Century

The former Roman field commander, Frankish king and founder of the Merovingian dynasty, Clovis I (466–511), annexed large tracts of Roman territory while uniting a series of previously independent Frankish war bands. From within his sixth-century Frankish kingdom two distinct zones emerged, broadly separated from one another by a notional line stretching from the mouth of the Loire, through the Saône to the Rhine.[3] The Loire and the Saône rivers effectively marked the division between the north and the south of the country. South of the Loire there was considerable continuity with the Roman past. Many of the old Roman landowning families still retained their estates, along with much of their culture and values. Two generations after Clovis, people in the south still spoke Latin, were conscious of their Roman senatorial heritage and retained an enduring interest in Roman culture.

There were hardly any signs at all of Frankish inward migration south of the Loire, and the basic Roman unit of local political, social and administrative life, the *civitas*, remained firmly in place. Only a few Frankish military garrisons were established, and the old elites repositioned themselves to the new demands of Frankish kings, but the degree of cultural and socioeconomic disruption was initially limited.

There were also important economic developments on the lower Rhône particularly, where Marseille had begun to replace Arles as the chief entry port for Mediterranean trade. Principally what had changed was that it was no longer possible for the aristocracy to follow bureaucratic careers that were formerly available in the Roman imperial administration. Success or failure now had to be fought-out at the royal courts of Clovis's Merovingian successors, the gateway for both major secular and ecclesiastical appointments.

North of the Loire, including the territories of present-day Belgium and the Rhineland, the situation was considerably different. Somewhere between 400 and 600, everyday life moved decisively away from the established norms of the Roman era.

As in lowland Britain by the late sixth century, the *civitas* as the stalwart of Roman administration had disappeared as a unit of political, social, economic and military organization. By the late sixth century, there is no evidence in these northern territories that military service was any longer organized on the basis of city contingents, as remained the case in the south.

Social and economic structures were also transformed. Legal sources indicate a society re-categorized, as in Anglo-Saxon England, but unlike Rome, into three social groups: the free; a class of permanent freedmen; and slaves. The second of these had not existed before in the Roman world. The Roman style of restricted aristocracy was replaced with a broader, less entrenched social elite – again, as in Anglo-Saxon England. The Church found itself the guardian and inheritor of Roman aristocratic values. Gregory, Bishop of Tours (538–94) does not refer to any major figure from north of the Loire as a 'noble', while he describes many from old Roman families south of the Loire in this way.[4] Gallo-Romans clearly formed part of the new ethnic mix that had emerged in these former Roman provinces by 600. This could have influenced how Augustine later dealt with the eclectic gathering of Christians at Saint Martin's oratory in Canterbury.

The Patrician Arigius

None of Gregory's surviving letters from his Papal *Regesta* relate to Augustine's first expedition into Provence. Also the sequence of Gregory's letters, written for the second expedition, may not indicate the order in which Augustine was able to meet with each of their recipients. However, the letters that the pope subsequently sent with Augustine on his return to Francia some months later do reveal his contacts in Provence during this period. These include Protasius, Bishop of Aix;[5] Abbot Stephen of Lérins;[6] and Arigius, the Patrician of Provence.[7]

By the last decade of the sixth century, Gallo-Roman senators and noblemen could be faced with a number of new challenges under their Merovingian rulers. In the north particularly, these included the final collapse of the vestiges of Roman municipal government; invasion by a new people (the Franks) who possessed a parallel aristocracy; and the emergence of a new kind of nobility based on holding office at Merovingian courts rather than on a senatorial class. At the courts of Metz, Chalon and Paris it was men of more humble birth than senators who had begun to take centre stage through their influence in the Frankish royal courts. By the latter part of the sixth century, possessing the *cingulum* (a heavy and decorated military belt) and being included in the table-fellowship of the Frankish kings counted for more than Roman senatorial family descent.

Both Gallo-Romans and Franks gravitated to positions of power and prestige, and the Franks sometimes accumulated great wealth along with the senators of former ancient Gaul. Alongside long-established senatorial families appeared more recent Frankish names such as Riculf, Ageric, Warnecher, Gundulf and Marilief.[8]

Roman concepts of service were joined to Germanic notions of allegiance to the person of the monarch, so that a cultural fusion was taking place at the courts of Merovingian monarchs throughout much of the sixth century. The most important accomplishments expected of a Frankish nobleman were still the skills of riding well and competence in handling weapons, but their power stemmed from their relationship to the kings, as well as being in possession of land and the number of servants and fighting men that they had at their command. The latter was important for securing influential votes at the annual March-fields army muster (a crucial political assembly) and were important in showing support for the king's military ventures.

The Burgundian kings had made the most of dynastic marriages; the aristocracy did the same. Those who constituted the seniors in the king's retinue counted for more than the senators, so that senatorial nobles no longer constituted the only aristocracy in Francia. In parallel with them and perhaps also through marriages of alliance between the two were members of the Frankish nobility who had followed in the train of the

Merovingian kings. Franks may have adopted Roman-sounding names, but some Gallo-Roman hopefuls may also have adopted Germanic names. What seems certain is that there was clear merit in imitating the conquerors.

Gregory's letter to Arigius asked for 'encouragement' for the group as they went through Gaul, presumably in the form of barges, baggage wagons and an armed escort. The title 'patrician' was a flexible term and seems to have been especially used in the Burgundian kingdom. Eastern Emperors gave the title to barbarian kings, and by the late sixth century 'patrician' could refer to an administrator of royal affairs in a large territory. As the designated Merovingian authority in the south, Arigius may have lived near to Marseille or more likely Aries, which was still the chief city of Provence.[9]

Arigius was already on friendly terms with Gregory before Augustine's mission. He had gathered the income from papal estates in Provence on the pope's behalf, overseen the transport and sale of produce and kept accurate accounts. He may also have looked after the interests of charitable institutions and the maintenance of monasteries and churches at Gregory's request. In this complex role Arigius functioned as one of Gregory's 'Rectors'.

As civil governor Arigius was clearly a member of the aristocracy and potentially a magnate whose extensive influence was of great assistance to Gregory, as it would be to Augustine. Few of the senatorial aristocracy were opposed to the Merovingians as a dynasty, and the relationship between the centre and the periphery in the kingdom was extremely complex. Both the Gallo-Roman aristocracy and their northern rulers exploited these relationships to their own advantage.

Bishop Protasius at Aquae Sextiae

Aquae Sextiae was founded in 123 BC by the Roman consul Sextius Calvinus, who gave his name to its springs and to the Thermae Sextii Roman baths built over them. However, by the sixth century the once ubiquitous Roman baths were in decline everywhere across the Roman Empire. Public baths had given way to the waters of baptism.

Entry through the southeastern gate of Aix would lead the missionaries past a small Jewish quarter to the forum on the north side of the city. Augustine's destination in Aix was Bishop Protasius. The bishop's episcopal palace was alongside Saint Saviour's Cathedral, on the northeast corner of the old forum. Church building under the Merovingians had largely continued the pattern of the Roman basilica. However, only a few small structures still remain, particularly baptisteries, and these had fallen out of fashion by the late sixth century and were not rebuilt.

Unlike Augustine's own basilica in Canterbury a few years later, none of the French cathedrals maintained a monastic community that shared a communal monastic life. Clergy or lay clerks, who sometimes lived separately within cathedral cloisters or otherwise took their own lodging in the town, supported their bishops. This throws light on Augustine's question to Gregory from Canterbury: should the bishop live separately from his clergy (as Frankish clergy did) or should he live with them, as a monastic community? Gregory insisted on the latter, which underscored a striking difference between English cathedrals and their Frankish counterparts from the early seventh century onwards.[10]

Crisis at Aquae Sextiae

By the time that Augustine arrived in Aix, it would have become abundantly clear that he lacked the most basic and essential element necessary to complete the journey through Francia, the pope's letters of introduction to open doors in high places. Abbot Stephen, Patrician Arigius and Bishop Protasius would all have drawn attention to this, leaving Augustine little choice – he would need to return to Rome and make good what he lacked.

Eyebrows would also have been raised that the pope had sent a monk instead of one of his bishops to conduct the mission to the *Angli*. Although Gregory had good reasons for this (he could not entrust his bishops with such a task), the status issue was nevertheless a significant one in a country where rank was the measure of a man and the importance of his task. Bishops conducted missions, not monks.

These two issues would have been sufficient reason for Augustine to return to Rome, but for Augustine's companions an even more compelling reason to return to Rome had arisen. Bede's account is the key record of this event – corroborated by Gregory's letter in response to the request of Augustine's companions to abandon the mission altogether – and shows that the missionaries' courage failed them, and Augustine's companions begged him to return to Rome and persuade the pope to abort the mission:

> Gregory, prompted by divine inspiration, sent a servant of God named Augustine and several more God-fearing monks with him to preach the word of God to the English race. In obedience to the pope's commands, they had already gone a little way on their journey when they were paralysed with terror. They began to contemplate returning home, rather than going to a barbarous, fierce and unbelieving nation whose language they did not even understand.[11]

Bede describes the mission as dangerous, wearisome and uncertain, which is an accurate enough description of what seems to have followed once their journey through Francia eventually resumed. Probably relying on an account provided by Abbot Albinus at Canterbury, Bede believed that the monks, having heard of the kind of reception that might greet them in England, lacked the courage to face the prospect of martyrdom. How might this rumour have taken such a strong hold on the hearts and minds of Augustine's companions?

It is worth considering the likely composition of the missionary group that accompanied Augustine and the direction from which this reaction came. Few monasteries in this period, including Saint Andrew's in Rome, would have had more than 25 'quire monks' in their community, those who had taken life profession and were submitted to the rule of their abbot. It is highly unlikely that Gregory would have committed nearly all of his monks to the mission. At most, Augustine's companions probably included half a dozen quire monks. Bede, together with his prime source Abbot Albinus, could name only two of Augustine's Roman companions: Peter, who became the first abbot of the newly formed abbey, and Laurence (Laurentius), who succeeded Augustine in Canterbury. Augustine and his small party of monks would have received hospitality at the bishop's own residence, but as there was no dormitory arrangement to accommodate the lay brothers, they would be billeted in the city. The townsfolk of Aix were an obvious source for gruesome tales of Anglo-Saxons, who had a reputation for military prowess in northern Francia.

Some of these accounts may have related to a group of Anglo-Saxons who had settled in Normandy and fought for the Neustrian King Chilperic against the Bretons. Others may have been more recent. Chilperic's widow, Queen Fredegund, also used these same Saxon warriors to fight alongside Bretons in a civil war against Brunhild, the dowager Queen of Austrasia. It is possible that this event took place only months before Augustine's arrival in Francia, so that rumours were rife around the town.[12]

Dissent was far more likely from among the group of lay brothers who accompanied Augustine than from his professed quire monks. The lay brothers had been former slaves on Gregory's family estate when the monastery was established. Their role on the mission would have been to assist with transporting the considerable baggage needed for their journey, as Augustine did not know precisely what resources might be needed in England. The lay brothers, chosen for their practical skills, would have regarded their service as distinct from the monastic calling of their companions, whose monastic vows included obedience, even to death. For Bede as chronicler of the mission, failure at this early stage must lie squarely with Augustine. However, fear of death was not the only or even the main reason for Augustine's return to Rome. In the light of subsequent events this seems unlikely. If encouragement for his companions was all that Augustine needed from the pope, the large number of additional letters that he carried on his return asking for support for the mission would have been unnecessary.

In addition to the letter from Gregory that Augustine carried back to his companions in Aix, Gregory also furnished Augustine with several other letters for ecclesiastical figures and rulers in Francia. Nearly all of these letters served the same purpose – to introduce Augustine as the pope's emissary and to seek material support for their journey through Francia.

Bede's loyalty to Gregory, always a heroic figure in his writings, made it impossible for him to consider an alternative explanation: that Augustine returned to Rome to remedy the pope's hasty and inadequate preparation for the mission that brought them into considerable difficulty in carrying out Gregory's charge. Subsequent events seem to confirm this. However, there is little doubt that Bede's description of the Anglo-Saxons as a barbarous, fierce and unbelieving nation was accurate for the sixth and most of the seventh century in England, including Bede's own Northumbria. Whether this was the situation in Kent during Aethelberht's reign appears unlikely, and what Augustine found on his arrival was quite different.

Re-evaluation

In considering the events that led to Augustine's return to Rome, it seems unlikely that he faced open rebellion from his companions. In all probability, as the royal house of Kent (speaking for the 'English people') had requested the mission, Augustine already anticipated that their ultimate arrival in Kent would be welcomed by the Anglo-Saxons and that they could expect hospitality from the royal court.

An alternative construction is that Augustine, after conversations with Abbot Stephen of Lérins, the Patrician Arigius and Bishop Protasius, took stock of the support they needed to continue the mission and found it substantially lacking. As the leader of the party Augustine returned to Gregory, but not to request the official abandonment of the mission. What Augustine needed most were letters of introduction for resources and assurances of support for the journey through Provence, Burgundy and northern Francia, and these he ultimately received.

What Augustine would have come to realize at Aix was that the northern churches were either less well disposed to Rome, less well organized than churches in the south, had less political influence with their civil rulers, or all of these combined. The factual statements in Bede's account of the mission are that Augustine was sufficiently concerned to return to Gregory and that he returned with the additional support from the pope that he needed.

Notes

1 In 655 Saint Augustine's Abbey in Canterbury received its first copy of Benedict's Rule from an Anglo-Saxon nobleman, Benedict Biscop. The copy was probably written at Lérins, where Biscop became a monk. In 664–5, Biscop, on his way to found the Northumbrian monasteries at Monkwearmouth and Jarrow, made his monastic profession at Lérins. Biscop chose the name Benedict as a mark of respect for Benedict of Norcia (c. 480–550) the author of the monastic Rule bearing his name.

2 Nicholas Brooks, *The Early History of the Church of Canterbury: Christ Church from 597 to 1066*, London and New York: Leicester University Press, 1984, p. 4.

3 Peter Heather, *Empires and Barbarians: Migration, Development and the Birth of Europe*, Oxford: Pan Books, 2009, p. 311.

4 Born in Clermont in the Auvergne district of central Gaul, Gregory of Tours was from the south.

5 Gregory the Great, Book VI, Letter 55.

6 Gregory the Great, Book VI, Letter 56.

7 Gregory the Great, Book VI, Letter 57.
8 Brian Brennan, 'Senators and social mobility in sixth-century Gaul', *Journal of Medieval History* 11:2 (1985), pp. 145–61.
9 Ian Wood, *Augustine's Journey*, Canterbury: Canterbury Chronicle, 1998, p. 28.
10 Bede, *Ecclesiastical History* I.27.
11 Bede, *Ecclesiastical History* I.26.
12 Miles Russell and Stuart Laycock, *UnRoman Britain: Exposing the Great Myth of Britannia*, Stroud: History Press, 2010, p. 207.

PART 2

Augustine in Francia

4

Return to Rome and Relaunch of the Mission

Augustine's return journey retraced his steps to Ostia, but this time most probably on a fully laden merchant vessel. His sailing companions probably included pilgrims (*peregrini*) to Rome, where Gregory had used the Church's considerable resources to set up food distribution centres for Rome's poor and also made special provision for pilgrims and visitors arriving in the Holy City. 'There were lots of them, and their numbers were growing. By the beginning of the seventh century Rome was ready to assume a new mantle: the premier pilgrimage destination of Christendom.'[1]

Neither Saint Andrew's Monastery nor Gregory's Lateran Basilica seem to have been directly involved in the relics aspect of the growing pilgrimage trade, as neither had saints or relics associated with their founding. Very few churches within the walls of Rome did have, and the major pilgrimage destinations, such as Saint Peter, Saint Paul, Saint Agnes and Saint Laurence, were all outside the city walls. As the seventh century wore on, the stream of pilgrims would grow into a flood, and chief among them was growing number of newly converted Anglo-Saxons, notably Bede's chief source of manuscripts, Benedict Biscop of Northumbria.

Augustine's return from Aix to Rome would also allow some time to reflect on his options for taking the mission forward. His status in Francia as *peregrinus*, a pilgrim and outsider with very limited rights in a foreign land, had left the mission in a highly vulnerable position. With no clear brief from Gregory, no letters of introduction and little access to much-needed resources, Augustine had been left to exert what personal authority he possessed to negotiate assistance along the way.

Once back in Rome, the last mile or so of the journey would be on foot past the Circus Maximus, abandoned since 549. Turning north at its eastern boundary would lead into an avenue running down the western side of the Caelian Hill, below the Colosseum. The last major event held there had taken place when Gregory was nine years old; now the entire block from the Circus Maximus to the Forum Romanum lay derelict, much as it appears today, a highly visible reminder of the transience of temporal power and the remorseless decline of the Western Empire. Another 100 yards along the avenue would bring the pope's emissary back to Saint Andrew's Monastery.

Augustine's Meeting with Gregory

A meeting with the pope took Augustine across the Caelian Hill by way of the narrow road Clivo di Scauro, past the Church of Saint John and Saint Paul (built over the house of two of Rome's earliest Christian martyrs) and down the Via di S. Stefano Rotondo to the Lateran Palace. The Lateran had been a gift from Constantine to the Bishop of Rome in the fourth century. Alongside it Constantine had erected the first of several new Christian basilicas in the city. Saint John in Lateran, the basilica of bishops of Rome, was built on the site of the barracks of the *Equites Singulares Augusti,* the Imperial Horse Guard, a special unit of around a thousand men. Constantine's way of punishing the Praetorian Guard for backing the wrong side in his battle against Maxentius – at a decisive battle near the Milvian Bridge on 28 October 312 – was to disband the Horse Guard and raze their barracks. A monastery was later built on the site, now attached to the south side of the basilica.

John the Deacon wrote a description of the pope who had commissioned Augustine: 'his beard of a rather tawny colour, rather bald, so that in the middle of his forehead he had two small neat curls, his darkish hair nicely curled and hanging down, his eyes had dark pupils, his nose thin and straight, slightly aquiline, his mouth was red, lips thick and subdivided, he had beautiful hands, with tapering fingers, well adapted for writing'.[2]

We can deduce the nature of Gregory's inquiries from the action that he took following his meeting with Augustine: What had precipitated his return? What was the welfare and mood of the monks? Was reaching England still feasible? What additional support, contacts, introductions and resources were needed to elicit support and protection through the Frankish territories?

It seems unlikely that Augustine returned to Rome simply to make a case for abandoning the mission. Gregory may for some years have nurtured plans for a mission to England, as Bede writes, but the details of the implementation are strikingly absent. The missionaries needed material support from influential rulers, both temporal and ecclesiastical, as well as interpreters for preaching to the Anglo-Saxons; protection, transport and much more besides. Up to this point, there is little evidence that Gregory made careful preparations for their route to Anglo-Saxon England. Gregory's subsequent letter to the Patrician Arigius was an attempt to make up for the absence of an initial introduction for Augustine's first meeting with the Provençal Governor. Gregory also widened the scope of their journey through Francia by adding the Roman Presbyter Candidus to their party, taking on the role of *vicedominus* who collected rents from papal lands in Provence. This would also have lengthened their journey and stay in Francia.

Of the British Church that Rome left behind in 410, Gregory evidently had no information at all. The pontiff's lack of current information concerning the British Church and the paucity of his contacts in Francia suggest a relatively thin network and little current information about conditions, particularly north of the Loire. Gregory's political and religious map, based on the Roman province of Britannia, was two centuries out of date. The archbishoprics of London and York no longer existed, whereas a sizeable British Church still survived, now mostly in Wales and also in Somerset and Cornwall. Population movements, the collapse of the Church and changes in local rulers and alliances were to render impractical much of the mission strategy as originally conceived.

Gregory's Response to the Abandonment of the Mission

If Augustine's companions in Aix were counting the cost of proceeding on a potentially fatal and fruitless mission, Gregory was working on a very different abacus in Rome. His response was that they should complete what they had set their hand to do. Crucially, Gregory was made aware that a higher status was essential for the mission, more a papal legation than a group of peripatetic monks. The latter had characterized Columbanus's mission to Burgundy a decade or so earlier.

The Kentish ruler was, after all, not a tribal savage but a sophisticated king connected to the Merovingian dynasty, and whose kingdom extended across much of southern England, perhaps as far as the Humber River. To increase their likelihood of success, Augustine needed credentials acceptable to the Canterbury court, and the role of monk – unknown in Anglo-Saxon England at this time, but certainly known to Bertha as a member of the Merovingian dynasty and of the Frankish Church – would by no means carry the requisite heft. The queen and royal court would need someone who could mount an effective mission to noble and peasant alike and who manifestly came with the full support of the Bishop of Rome.

If Gregory had initially intended that Augustine merely establish a bridgehead in Canterbury until a suitable bishop could be sent from Rome, this was radically revised at their meeting in the Lateran. Looking ahead, Gregory would also have recognized the need to consecrate bishops for London, Rochester and ideally York, but persuading reluctant Frankish bishops to cross the English Channel to do this could be problematic. Gregory found a solution. Among his mission correspondence, copied by

Nothelm for Bede,[3] was a request to the Bishop of Arles to consecrate Augustine as bishop on his return to Provence.

The pope was clearly adamant that the mission should continue, and once alerted to its needs, Gregory took a number of decisive steps. He expected that monasteries en route would provide hospitality for the missionaries and that bishops would provide for their travel and safety; and in extreme circumstances, Candidus could make use of funds from the papal patrimony rents due to Rome. However, the distribution of the letters indicates that Gregory's ecclesiastical contacts ceased at the banks of the Saône and the Loire. Safe passage to the English Channel could also require the active participation of different Frankish rulers, and that might be more difficult to secure.

Gregory's Letters and the Papal *Regesta*

Our knowledge of Gregory's contribution to Augustine's mission is drawn substantially from his Papal *Regesta* (from Latin *regerere*, to inscribe) – a special registry of volumes of the pope's letters and official documents held in the papal archives. Some archival collections pre-date Constantine's conversion to Christianity and were an important source of authority in the Church's doctrinal disputes (such as the date of Easter). They seem always to have been held by the Church in Rome. Gregory's archive of nearly 850 letters for the period 590–604 is one of the few *Regesta* collections to have survived from before the twelfth century. Conflagrations and warfare in the city have accounted for the loss of the oldest records.

Gregory's original *Regesta* consisted of 14 papyrus volumes, corresponding to the years of his pontificate and arranged according to Roman 15-year cycles ('indictions'). Each of these volumes was divided into 12 parts, and at the beginning of each part the name of the corresponding month was inscribed.[4] Gregory's letters written in support of Augustine's mission were initially dictated to his scribes, who used a shorthand notation originally ascribed to Tiro, Cicero's slave and scribe (c. 63 BC) to swiftly record information by using fewer symbols. To learn the Tironian notation system scribes required formal schooling in some 13,000 symbols. In receiving dictation from Gregory, scribes first captured the words in shorthand on wax tablets and then prepared a full text on papyrus. Copies were also made for the Papal *Regesta* before dispatch in the form of a papyrus scroll.

Book VI.51 is Gregory's first letter dealing explicitly with the mission. It confronts his and Augustine's most urgent problem – the fears and the resolve of the group of monks and lay brothers left in Aix and anxiously awaiting Augustine's return. Bede included a copy of this letter in *Ecclesiastical History* I.23. Gregory informed the missionaries that they should persevere because of the inherent worthiness of the task and stressed the potential spiritual rewards. To make Augustine's leadership position unambiguous to the missionaries, Gregory made him their *praepositus* (literally 'prior'), calling for absolute obedience from the members of his party.

As all of Gregory's letters from VI.51 to VI.59 relate directly to the re-launch of the mission, it seems that the pope composed them in rapid succession, undistracted by other correspondence and perhaps while Augustine was present to confer on the details. Most of the letters in this series are to bishops whom Augustine might be expected to meet en route to England. Letters that contained the same message – which was the case for letters to several of the bishops – were not duplicated in Gregory's *Regesta*; instead, all the names of the intended recipients are grouped together at the beginning of the archived letter.

It seems that most of the letters relating to the mission were intended to elicit support for Augustine's journey rather than to prescribe the route that he should follow. The crucial exceptions were letters to Theudebert II and Theuderic II (VI.58) and also the last letter relating to the mission, VI.59. This was addressed to Brunhild, dowager queen and grandmother of the two young kings. The pope addressed her as 'Queen of the Franks'. These letters would be essential for Augustine to obtain interpreters for the missionary effort and a passage to Canterbury.

A further indication of Gregory's greater attention to the details of the mission following Augustine's return to Rome is evident in the books that Augustine was given to take with him to England. 'Augustine must have had books containing the prayers, readings and directions for Mass throughout the year, in addition to a Roman calendar, martyrology, and hymnal.'[5]

It is also highly probable that Augustine brought with him Gregory's own *Regula Pastoralis* (Pastoral Rule). At the beginning of his pontificate Gregory had written this Rule for his bishops, and this now had clear relevance for Augustine as the first missionary–bishop to Kent. It seems clear that '[i]f there had been a crisis in Augustine's leadership and resolve, the fact that after meeting with Gregory he was willing and able to lead the party onwards without further incident suggests that the crisis was effectively surmounted'.[6]

Augustine's Return to Provence

Returning to Francia as late as September would carry increasing risks from the Mistral growing in severity, so that fewer ships would undertake the journey from Ostia to Francia. It would also have become clear that the missionaries would not leave Francia for England for another six or seven months, until spring in 597, relieving some of the pressure on the pace of their travel.

Although Francia features significantly in Gregory's documentation for Augustine's mission, Bede knew nothing of the details within the country and only records: 'So Augustine, strengthened by the encouragement of St Gregory, in company with the servants of Christ, returned to the work of preaching the word, and came to Britain.'[7]

The gap in Bede's record amounts to about ten months, and he appears unaware of any difficulties that the monks might have faced during this period. Since many of Gregory's remedial steps following Augustine's return were concerned with precisely this, it is a significant gap in Bede's account.

Based on the distribution of Gregory's letters in support of the mission, the first stage of Augustine's return journey took place in the once independent kingdom of the Burgundians. These East German tribesmen had been strong allies of Rome for more than a century until the conquest and annexation of Burgundy in 554 by the northern Franks under Charibert I, Queen Bertha's father. Lyon had been the capital of the Burgundian kingdom. As the geographical distribution of Gregory's correspondence confirms, the co-operation of Frankish rulers was to prove essential to the mission.

At the same time, a chief source of the difficulties the missionaries faced was the growing political instability both within and between the kingdoms of Neustria and Austrasia. This had roots in events nearly 35 years before Augustine's arrival.

Rivalry between Rulers: Brunhild and Fredegund

The rivalries and conflicts between Chilperic, Sigibert, Guntram and Charibert, all sons and successors of Chlothar I (d.561), were to become the hallmark of the Merovingian dynasty for the next 50 years. All four kings were dead by 592. Sigibert and Brunhild's son, Childebert II, died in March 596. This left two sons, both minors, to succeed him. The country was plunged into yet another round of political and military instability. By the summer of 596 the most influential players left on the Merovingian stage were two dowager queens: Fredegund of Neustria, guardian of her 13-year-old son Chlothar II; and Brunhild, who ruled as regent over Austrasia and Burgundy for her two grandsons, of both similar age to Chlothar.

Gregory was aware of Childebert's death even before he launched Augustine's mission in 596, but he was not aware of its political consequences. Fredegund and her Neustrian advisers seized the opportunity presented by Childebert's death to occupy the city of Paris, a neutral city since Charibert's death in 567, making it her son Chlothar's new capital city. A year later Brunhild and her Austrasian inner circle retaliated by declaring war on Neustria, by now a relatively small territory comprising only 12 cantons between the Loire, the Oise and the sea.[8] Brunhild's declaration of war may have been made early in March 597, at the time that kings traditionally met with their warriors and decided whether to go to war. However, Brunhild and her advisers were wrong-footed by Fredegund, whose war band defeated the Austrasian forces at Laffau in Picardie through a cunning stratagem of deception.

One implication is that, even as Augustine and his companions were preparing for their final leg of the journey through Neustria to the English Channel, northern Francia was preparing for war between the two rival Merovingian kingdoms. This could only heighten any concern for their safety, as well as cause greater difficulty in finding material support such as transport and food (people hoard against times of shortage), shelter and protection.

Also, judging from the distribution of Gregory's correspondence, it seems that the pope had no loyal ecclesiastical contacts in northern Francia. If Augustine made any contact north of the Loire with Fredegund or Chlothar II, this was at his own initiative, not by direction from the pope. In terms of diplomacy, Gregory's close association with Brunhild would have made contact extremely difficult.

Îles de Lérins to Marseille

Augustine's return journey together with the priest Candidus may have been almost identical to the first – from Rome to Ostia and Ostia to Lérins to deliver the pope's first letter relating to the expedition. Gregory thanked Abbot Stephen for his gifts – spoons and plate – brought by Augustine on his return to Rome.[9] Augustine probably sailed to Marseille from Lérins to make up some lost time. The port of Marseille (*Masilia*) was the oldest and largest trading emporium in ancient Gaul, a legacy of Greek–Phoenician traders who had settled below the Rhône some 1200 years earlier. The port city was a polyglot of languages and ethnic groups – Greeks, Romans, Visigoths and Franks, traders, aristocrats and slaves.

John Cassian (365–435), one of the most significant influences on the monastic movement in late Roman Antiquity, founded two monasteries in Marseille: the Monastery for men became the Abbey of Saint Victor in 415, and the present crypt of the abbey held the bones of the first Christian martyrs in Marseille. Gregory of Tours noted that by the last decade of the sixth century a large basilica was consecrated to Saint Victor the Martyr attracting numerous pilgrims, and miracles began to be reported at the saint's tomb. Augustine could not have failed to notice the basilica as he sailed into the old port.

There is no letter in Gregory's Papal *Regesta* to the Abbot of Saint Victor for Augustine to deliver in 596, but it is far more likely that Augustine met with Bishop Serenus (596–601), then newly appointed to the See of Marseille, on his return to Provence. Gregory's letter (VI.52) to the bishop is one of two identical letters sent in support of Augustine's mission; the other was addressed to Pelagius of Tours (*Turni*). There is no suggestion in Gregory's letter to Serenus that he had met Augustine during the missionary's first journey to Provence earlier in 596.

Within a few years Gregory would be writing again to Serenus, this time to reprove him for his excessive iconoclastic zeal. Serenus had entered several churches in Marseille and broken down their images of Christ. Gregory commended Serenus's fervour against idolatry, but reproved his violence, since representations of Christ in a church were used so that the illiterate might read from the walls what they were unable to read for themselves in the Scriptures. As Augustine carried an icon in his baggage en route to England, we can assume that it was for just this purpose. That he was in possession of such an item would have made any close rapport with Serenus extremely difficult.

Gregory's letter to Serenus requested support for Augustine and Candidus in their respective ventures. The most immediate assistance they needed was to travel the 15 miles from Marseille to Aix to rejoin Augustine's companions, requiring perhaps two days' journey on foot or less than a day on horseback.

Return to Aquae Sextiae

Augustine needed significant support from the Frankish Church. Bishop Protasius of Aix was clearly one such supporter. Like Arigius, he had previously acted as Gregory's *vicedominus* in southern Francia, responsible for the Papal Patrimony in Provence. While Gregory's letters of introduction to bishops and other influential people would prove essential for the mission, the detailed negotiations fell to Augustine. His party needed to be strengthened by the addition of Frankish priests, both as interpreters and as evangelists to minister among the Anglo-Saxons. Much of the route now taken by Augustine reflects his attempt to secure a safe passage and the resources he needed to reach England.

On his return from Rome, Augustine called his missionaries together and read them the pope's exhortation. Gregory's letter began in customary style:

Gregory, servant of the servants of God, to the servants of the Lord.

My dearly beloved sons, it would have been better not to have undertaken a noble task than to turn back deliberately from what you have begun: so it is right that you should carry out with all diligence this good work which you have begun with the help of the Lord. Therefore do not let the toilsome journey nor the tongues of evil speakers deter you. But carry out the task you have begun under the guidance of God with all constancy and fervour . . . When Augustine your prior returns, now, by our appointment, your abbot, humbly obey him in all things . . . May Almighty God protect you by his grace and grant that I may see the fruit of your labours in our heavenly home . . . I hope to share in the joy of your reward. May God keep you safe, my dearly beloved sons.[10]

The pope had given the lay brothers manumission from slavery on his own estate in Rome, a place within his monastic community and a new role as freed men. He had renounced his own considerable property rights and joined them, not as their former pater familias now returned in the guise of abbot but as a brother in Christ. He knew each one personally. They owed him everything. Now as their bishop and supreme head of the Catholic Church, who had commissioned them for this journey, he was asking them to return to their labours. For all these reasons, they could not refuse him.

The journey continued.

The Presbyter Candidus

Candidus, appointed by Gregory to act as *vicedominus* of the Papal Patrimony in Francia, was commended to Arigius by letter, which clearly indicates the pope's intention that Augustine should meet with Arigius a second time. It is not clear at what stage or where on Augustine's second journey through Provence this meeting took place, but possibly in the region of Arles because of its key location on the Rhône. Gregory's letter to Arigius concludes:

> Furthermore, we commend to you in all respects our son the presbyter Candidus, whom we have sent for the government of the patrimony of our Church which is in your parts; trusting that your Glory will receive a reward in return from our God, if with devout mind you lend your succour to the concerns of the poor.[11]

In a similar manner Candidus is introduced to Brunhild in a letter Augustine carried to the dowager queen. This suggests that the presbyter accompanied the missionary party throughout their journey in Provence and Burgundy, if not further. It also indicates that Gregory's interests in the Patrimony of Saint

Peter extended beyond Provence to Burgundy and perhaps into the heartland of the Frankish kingdom. There may have been pockets of land given to the Roman Church in other parts of Francia that had escaped papal attention for some considerable time. None of these revenues would directly alleviate problems in Rome, but they would provide papal resources for (almost entirely monastic) education and alleviate poverty within Francia itself.

If Candidus received payments in coin from those who supervised the papal lands on their route, the protection offered by a large group of companions would have been essential. It is also possible that Arigius provided an armed escort from his own resources. This also raises the prospect that Augustine requested armed escorts even from bishops during his journey. In any event, the decision to seek protection of this kind would have rested with Augustine. It is an open question whether prudence or trust in God directed his decision.

From Aix to Arles (*Arelate*)

Departing from Aix, the missionaries travelled westward to Arles, Roman *Arelate*. Their route would have continued on the *Via Aurelia* from Aquae Sextiae through the present-day villages and rural towns of Salon-de-Provence, Eyguières, Mouries and Mausanne-les-Alpilles, then beneath the Roman aqueduct from Alpilles through Les Baux-de-Provence and Fontveille for the last few miles before arriving at Arles after a total distance of some 45 miles (72 km).

Despite the rise of Marseille in the sixth century, Arles remained a key commercial centre on the Rhône, a polyglot city of travellers, merchants and traders from northern Europe, the Mediterranean, Spain and the east. Pilgrims who thronged the roads in the late sixth century would be ubiquitous, particularly those in search of relics that related to Saint Martin.

Augustine's Consecration as Bishop

Arles, owing to its situation on the Rhône, was the obvious place for the missionaries to begin their passage north. For Gregory it was expedient to have Augustine consecrated as bishop in Francia, as this would help to cement both Frankish ecclesiastical and royal support for the mission; and specifically in Arles, a symbolic act that acknowledged the ancient arch-episcopal oversight that Arles once exercised over former Britannia. While this conferred no Frankish rights over the future English Church, it was an astute political gesture.

The Cathedral of Saint-Etienne was erected a short distance from the southeast corner of the forum, and here Augustine was consecrated by Bishop Virgilius (588–613). However, according to Bede, 'Augustine went to Arles and, in accordance with the command of Pope Gregory, was consecrated archbishop of the English race *by Etherius*, the archbishop of that city.'[12] Bede's record of Augustine's consecration seems confused at two points. Firstly, Etherius was Bishop of Lyon at this time, not Arles, whose bishop was Virgilius. However, this does not preclude Etherius, who was Primate of all Gaul, from being present in Arles for Augustine's consecration, and Etherius's participation in the event may possibly be the source of Bede's confusion.[13]

Secondly, Bede places this event *after* Augustine's arrival in England, not en route to Kent. However, it seems more credible that Augustine was consecrated as bishop before his arrival in England in 597 and not at a later time, as Bede believed. In Bede's sequence of events, Augustine would have been consecrated a bishop between 598 and 601, which would have entailed an unnecessary and lengthy return to Francia from Kent just as the mission was beginning to expand dramatically.[14]

Against Bede's sequence of events is a letter from Gregory to Bertha that already refers to Augustine as a fellow bishop in 598–9. In placing Augustine's consecration as late as 601, Bede seems to confuse Augustine's consecration as bishop with receiving the pallium from Gregory, which conferred the office of Archbishop of Canterbury on Augustine. Receiving the pallium required no additional act of consecration, and it was no doubt brought to Augustine by Laurentius and Peter.

Probability also leans towards Arles as the place of Augustine's consecration for a more pragmatic reason. A year before the launch of Augustine's mission to England Gregory had already corresponded with the Bishop of Arles. In 595 Virgilius had written to Gregory requesting that he be appointed papal vicar and allowed to use the pallium. The King of Austrasia, Childebert II, who had ruled most of Francia since 593, had also supported this request. Gregory granted Virgilius the pallium, but seized the opportunity to secure the king's backing for his reforms within the Frankish Church. Gregory asked Childebert to put a stop to the 'heresy' of simony, as well as the consecration of aristocratic laymen as bishops, practices in which the Austrasian crown was deeply implicated.[15] Virgilius, having received the pallium from Gregory, could not easily refuse the pope's request to consecrate Augustine as bishop.

In many respects, Augustine appeared to be an anomaly: unlike the Frankish bishops, he was not from a well-connected aristocratic background, nor did he acquire his consecration through royal preferment or simony. He was a monk sworn to a life of poverty and celibacy, consecrated entirely on merit for the role of missionary–bishop to the *Angli*, for which there was no cathedra awaiting him in Canterbury. Gregory's intention for Augustine's consecration was both ecclesiastically symbolic and politically astute and affirmed the growing importance of monasticism in the emerging Roman Church, linking it closely with the changing ecclesiastical landscape in Rome.

Notes

1 Matthew Sturgis, *When in Rome: 2000 Years of Roman Sightseeing*, London: Frances Lincoln Limited (Kindle book), 2011, p. 1089.

2 Christopher Donaldson, *The Great English Pilgrimage: From Rome to Canterbury*, Norwich: Canterbury Press, 1995, p. 4.

3 Bede, *Ecclesiastical History* I.27.

4 J. P. Kirsch, 'Papal Regesta', *The Catholic Encyclopaedia*, New York: Robert Appleton Company, 1911, available at: www.newadvent.org/cathen/12715a.htm.

5 R. Gameson (ed.), *St Augustine and the Conversion of England*, Stroud: Sutton Publishing Ltd, 1999, p. 313.

6 Gameson, *St Augustine*, p. 10.

7 Bede, *Ecclesiastical History* I.25.

8 Ian Wood, 'Augustine and Gaul', in Gameson, *St Augustine*, p. 68.

9 Gregory the Great, Book VI, Letter 56.

10 Bede, *Ecclesiastical History* I. 23.

11 Gregory the Great, Book VI, Letter 57.

12 Bede, *Ecclesiastical History* I.27.

13 It would not be an unreasonable assumption for Bede to make, that the Primate of all Gaul was the person to consecrate Augustine. However, as Augustine would need to pass through Lugdunum (Lyon) on his way to England, there would be less compulsion for Etherius to make the long and hazardous journey to Arles.

14 Gameson, *St Augustine*, p. 372.

15 Marilyn Dunn, *The Christianization of the Anglo-Saxons c. 597–c. 700: Discourses of Life, Death and Afterlife*, London: Continuum, 2009, p. 48.

5

Arles to Autun

The Rhône was a vital inland route for trade and travel, a major artery connecting the cities of Arles, Avignon, Valence, Vienne and Lyon to the Mediterranean ports of Fos, Marseille and Sete. Navigation was difficult. The Rhône suffered then as now from fierce currents and treacherous shallows, floods in spring and early summer when the ice melts and droughts in late summer. The less turbulent Saône connects the Rhône ports to the cities of Villefranche-sur-Saône, Mâcon and Chalon-sur-Saône, which was one of Augustine's most significant destinations in Francia.

From sea level at Marseille the Rhône rises to an altitude of 170 metres at Lyon and by a further 18 metres to reach Chalon-sur-Saône. Cataracts are numerous, and without locks on the waterways transporting boats and goods overland would be required to make progress upstream. Even given the prevalence of slave labour, human as well as transport logistics would be considerable in maintaining commerce along this route.

Travelling the Rhône downstream by barge could take three weeks and longer travelling upstream. Traders used *barques du Rhône*, large sailing barges that required as many as 50–80 horses to haul trains of five to seven barges upstream. Passengers such as Augustine and his companions travelled in smaller *coches d'eau* (water coaches) drawn by both men and horses, under sail or even on the backs of donkeys along the towpaths.

Valence and Vienne

A number of ancient Gallo-Roman cities line the Rhône between Arles and Lyon. Vienne became a major urban centre and a Roman provincial capital, as well as an important early bishopric in Christian Gaul. Julius Caesar transformed the city in 47 BC from the ancient Gallic community of the Allobroges into a Roman colony. Much of the *romanitas* of daily life exhibited in Roman Gaul in 596, by this time part of Merovingian Francia for nearly a century, continued uninterrupted. The public buildings that Augustine saw were of stone and in a superior condition compared to Rome's stripped-down brick and concrete structures.

Vienne's richly appointed villas with fine mosaic floors occupied the best views on both sides of the Rhône. Busy warehouses stretched along the banks of the river, supporting a thriving commercial trade between the Mediterranean south and Lyon, Chalon and Metz to the northeast and as far as Orléans and Tours on the Loire to the west. The city's Gallo-Roman structures still standing today would have been part of Augustine's landscape in Vienne: the cathedral, dedicated at that time to the Maccabee brothers; the Temple of Augustus and Livia, adopted as a church from the early Middle Ages; the amphitheatre, possibly little used by the end of the sixth century, but one of the largest in the Roman world and dominating the hillside above the town and the sixth-century Church of Saint Peter.

Bishop Desiderius of Vienne, whose episcopal palace lay within a complex of buildings close to the cathedral, was the next after Arles to receive a letter by hand from Augustine. Desiderius was a noted chronicler and theologian appointed to his post with the support of King Guntram of Burgundy. At its height in 587 Guntram's *Regnum Burgundiae* briefly commanded the greater part of Gaul, including Bordeaux, Rennes and Paris, in addition to Gundobad's former Kingdom of Burgundy.[1] Guntram bequeathed his kingdom to Brunhild's son Childebert in 592.

Desiderius was a recipient of one of Gregory's letters in which the pope commended to the bishop not only Augustine but also his travelling companion, Candidus. As Rector of the Papal Patrimony, Candidus had charge of all the papal estates owned by the Roman Church in southern Francia, and these included estates in Vienne.[2]

Desiderius was not one of Brunhild's favourites; she had not appointed him to his see (this fell to King Guntram), but also the relationship between Church and Crown decisively changed under her rule. The bishop's position became increasingly tenuous as his relationship with Queen Brunhild deteriorated. The queen was a dangerous ally and an implacable foe. She brought to trial Abbot Lupentius (Abbot of Javols) on a charge of *lèse-majesté* – offending against the dignity of the sovereign. Lupentius was acquitted of the charge, but murdered while returning to Javols.

A few years after receiving Augustine, Bishop Desiderius, together with the fiery and charismatic Irish monk Columbanus, would take the risky step of castigating Theuderic II (the young King of Burgundy and Brunhild's grandson) for fathering offspring out of wedlock. Retaliation soon followed. Theuderic and Brunhild used the Council of Chalon to depose Desiderius in 603. He was murdered in 611, around the time that Theuderic and Brunhild also drove Columbanus out of his monastery at Luxeuil and from Francia altogether. At Chalaronne, where Desiderius was martyred, miraculous cures soon began to be reported.

Lyon *(Lugdunum)*

By tradition the settlement of Lugdunum, some 30 km north of Vienne on the Rhône, was named after the Celtic god Lug. The *'dunum'* may have referred to a fort built by Roman conquerors in 43 BC. Until the end of the fourth century Lugdunum was one of the most important centres in the Western Roman Empire. The city, lying at the confluence of the Saône and Rhône, first developed on the Fourvière Hill (*Forum Vetus*, Old Forum), where a forum, theatre, temple of Cybele, Odeum and public baths were erected. The city was also located at the intersection of major Roman roads; four aqueducts carried the settlement's water supply, and their ruins can still be seen in the region.

Two important features of sixth-century Lugdunum differed from the present landscape. The Peninsula (Presqu'île) that lies between the Rhône and the Saône was, in the late sixth century, an island cut off from the mainland by a branch of the Rhône that flowed into the Saône. The two rivers joined where the Presqu'île now rises steeply towards the Amphitheatre of the Three Gauls. The island was also about half the length of the present Peninsula.

Lyon is also by tradition the birthplace of Christianity in Gaul. In 177 Lyon witnessed the death of 48 martyrs in the amphitheatre of the Three Gauls, situated on a south-facing hill above the Peninsula. These persecutions marked the beginning of Lugdunum's change in fortunes, and by the fourth century the Roman Church had grown in power to become the official religion of the Empire. The archdiocese of Lyon dates to this period, and the Archbishop of Lyon still holds the title of Primate of the Gauls as the leading archbishop in France.

Lyon's key position came to an end with the collapse of Roman administration in Gaul after the fall of Rome in 410. Troops were withdrawn to protect Italy, and Gaul ceased to be a Roman province. Lugdunum shrank to a small area along the banks of the Saône. Visigoths, Burgundians and Franks filled this power vacuum in the years between 455 and 476. Within the sixth century the Roman Church in Francia under the Merovingian dynasty became a powerful force. However, the former primacy of Lyon also came under threat, not from the destruction of war or the interference of the State, but from the rise of other churches across Francia – Reims, Arles, Vienne, Orléans, Tours, Autun, Paris and others.

Augustine and his companions arrived in a city that breathed an atmosphere of uncertainty; Lyon was no longer special.

Augustine's Meeting with Metropolitan Etherius

Although Etherius as Archbishop of Lyon was officially styled the Primate of all Gaul, in reality the city and the archdiocese were considerably diminished after the collapse of Roman rule. In contrast, the church in Vienne and commercial trade associated with the city had overshadowed its neighbour upstream. Until the ninth century the shrinking population of Lyon hugged the right bank of the Saône in small communities that dotted the hillsides and a narrow stretch of the left bank. The town remained divided between religious and secular followers: a district frequented by craftsmen and merchants sprang up to the north, around Saint-Paul, where a Jewish community had begun to form, similar to Arles. However, the fluctuating fortunes of both city and church influenced attitudes, and in 846 Jewish merchants were accused by the Archbishop of Lyon of looking no further than Provence for their source of supply of slaves and of selling Christian slaves to traders in Cordoba.[3]

The fourth-century cathedral Saint-Jean-Baptiste and its associated churches Holy Cross and Saint-Etienne comprised the heart of the town on a small island on the western bank of the Saône. These buildings towered in the centre of a fortified enclosure around the archepiscopal palace, a prison, the cloister and living quarters of the canons. A baptistery, now a ruin, stood immediately to the north of the cathedral. (Sainte-Croix and Saint-Etienne were destroyed during the French Revolution; only their ruins remain.)

There can be little doubt that Augustine and the Metropolitan of Lyon did in fact meet. Bede had a copy of a letter addressed to Etherius (identical to the letters the pope wrote to Bishop Serenus and also to Pelagius of Tours), and the most likely place for Augustine's companions to lodge while passing through Lyon was the archbishop's palace and the accommodation provided for his canons.

As metropolitan, Etherius would not only have welcomed the missionaries, but also have ensured that Augustine's arrival at Chalon-sur-Saône was anticipated. It was important to keep Brunhild informed of the movements of significant foreign visitors through her domain, and the archbishop would have given what support he could to secure an audience with Brunhild. However, as Augustine embarked on the next and crucial stage of his journey up the Saône, he would have no certainty of finding any of the three Merovingian rulers, to whom he carried Gregory's letters, conveniently waiting to receive him. The early Merovingian kings were well endowed with former Roman estates and palaces, some of these once part of the Roman Imperial Treasury. The royals were often to be found on their estates, rather than in their cities, giving judgement or dispensing grants from a palace or royal villa, but mostly absorbed in hunting pursuits and feasting. Delays brought about by events such as these could go some way in explaining the extended length of time that Augustine's journey took through Francia.

Lyon to Chalon-sur-Saône (*Cabyllona*)

The journey from Lyon to Chalon-sur-Saône may have taken up to two weeks or so by barge, hauled upstream against the Saône by teams of oxen. Chalon is situated above the Saône Valley, strategically located on the border between Austrasia and Burgundy and at one time the demarcation between northern and southern Francia. The city was once located at a major crossroads and initially served as Julius Caesar's supply depot during his Gallic campaigns. Chalon had been a suffragan see of the Archdiocese of Lyon since Roman times. Agricola, a bishop from a senatorial family, built the original Cathedral of Saint-Vincent in 570–80.

There was little prospect of Augustine meeting Queen Brunhild en route from Lyon. Merovingian kings and queens rarely travelled south of the Loire–Saône rivers; they favoured large estates and palaces so that their itineraries were centred in the north. Throughout the fourth century Trier and the entire Moselle valley had remained a hub of prosperous *romanitas* in town, country and culture. The city itself had been an imperial capital for several years. The region between the Rhine and the Loire, as a whole, had not been abandoned by the Empire, as was the case in most of Gaul, and an active Roman life still continued across much of it.[4]

The Austrasian branch of the Merovingian dynasty initially had its seat at Trier, a former Roman capital, but by the third quarter of the sixth century this had relocated to Metz. A second-division town such as Metz presented an easier canvas upon which to inscribe the dynasty's own political identity. The Merovingians created a royal complex that had all the elements of an imperial palace – audience chamber, major church and arena. This was important as Trier possessed its own self-confident local aristocracy that was based on the *civitas* and stressed its *romanitas*. This, combined with an awkward local episcopal tradition of bishops standing up to secular power, made the old Roman imperial city difficult to adapt to a new and upcoming regime.

Chalon assumed importance as a royal centre once King Guntram had relocated his capital from Orléans. On his death in 592 Guntram had bequeathed the city and all Burgundy to his nephew Childebert II, Brunhild's son. Perhaps because of her earlier painful associations with Metz, Brunhild and Childerbert adopted Chalon as their capital city. The *castrum* (fortified walled enclosure) of Chalon-sur-Saône was already politically significant during the early Merovingian period, and after the division of the Merovingian kingdom in 561 King Guntram made frequent visits to the town. Theuderic II (596–613) also made Chalon his main royal residence in Frankish Burgundy.

Little is known of the topography of the city in the high Middle Ages, apart from its semi-elliptical walls that were common to Roman towns in the late Roman Empire. Built on the upper bank of the Saône, Chalon's *castrum* hosted a cathedral on the eastern side of the enclosure, and Guntram's private chapel and palace occupied the southwest corner. Outside the city wall, to the southwest, and on the edge of the Saône, a leper colony was served by Saint-Jean-de-Mézel, built by Bishop Agricola around 580.[5]

Augustine's party may have received hospitality from the abbot at Saint Marcellus while Augustine and Candidus prepared for their audience with the queen. The church and monastery of Saint Marcellus situated two and a half miles to the southeast of the city was founded by Guntram, and the practice of perpetual chant was first instituted there. Guntram died at the age of 67 and was buried in the church. Almost immediately he was declared a saint by his subjects. Of his relics only the skull remains, and the monastic buildings were reduced to ruins by the tenth century.

Brunhild as dowager queen ruled from within the ancient *castrum* that defined the old town. If the extravagant opulence of other Merovingian royal courts is any guide, it is possible to envisage what may also have existed at Chalon. Arranged around the main body of the palace would be the dwellings of the mayor of the palace and officers and the chiefs of warrior companies who had sworn an oath of loyalty to the queen. Families of tradesmen, manufacturers of arms, jewellery, clothing and all the essentials demanded by a royal establishment occupied lesser houses.

The circuit of Chalon's walls indicates that the Cathedral of Saint-Vincent, its cloister, and the episcopal quarters were all integrated into this arrangement. The incumbent bishop in 596 was Flavius and apparently not Brunhild's favourite; this was reserved for Bishop Syagrius of Autun. Outside this walled enclosure farm buildings and cottages for labourers and slaves served the royal estate, together with barns, sheepfolds, cattle stalls and paddocks, so that the overall impression of Chalon was that of an ancient Germanic village, much like those found east of the Rhine.[6]

During the sixth century the Merovingian Franks had appropriated most of the gold and silver furnishings of the former Gallo-Roman rulers. They divided what was left among their aristocrats, chieftains and warriors as 'spoils of war'. In this way over the next few centuries the recycled remains of the late Roman Empire found their way into Frankish palaces, cathedrals and monasteries. As dowager Queen of both Austrasia (which included Belgium and the Rhineland) and Burgundy (territories south of the Saône and east of the Rhône), Brunhild's dominion embraced nearly all of the Merovingian kingdoms except for Neustria. Through these the Queen had access to substantial public coffers, as well as her considerable personal wealth. Taxes imposed on key maritime trading centres, such as Dorestad in the north, also contributed to her purse.

It seems likely that a very high level of luxury and comfort was displayed at Chalon. Merchants brought a steady stream of the most costly items from every quarter of the Mediterranean world.[7] Goods were drawn into the maw of Chalon from Cologne and Belgium; from Trier, Paris and Autun, Lyon and Vienne, Arles and the Mediterranean; from Rome and Ostia; from Cadiz in Spain; from North Africa, Carthage and Alexandria; from the eastern Mediterranean, Athens, Ephesus, Constantinople, the Black Sea, Crete and Palestine in the Middle East. These fed an insatiable appetite for luxuries in jewellery, tableware, linens, textiles and carvings to satisfy one of the wealthiest global shoppers, Queen Brunhild, second only to the Empress Constantina herself.

Yet, despite her external trappings of wealth and power, Brunhild's position in the royal court was far from secure.

Brunhild's Support for the Mission

A Visigoth princess and a staunch Catholic, Brunhild had married King Sigibert of Austrasia in 567. Sigibert was murdered in 575 (Queen Fredegund of Neustria is regarded as the most likely perpetrator). According to custom their son and heir Childebert II was made king while still a minor, but Brunhild found herself exiled to Rouen by the mayor of the Austrasian palace and separated from her son for the next few years. After a disastrous political marriage to her nephew Merovech, who was the son and rival of her half-brother-in-law Chilperic of Neustria, Brunhild was grudgingly re-admitted to the Austrasian court. She gradually strengthened her position once

Childebert became king in his own right in 583. Mother and son formed an effective alliance for the next 13 years until Childebert's unexpected death in March 596, so that by the time Augustine arrived in Chalon in the autumn of that year, Brunhild's position was once more precarious.

Childebert had been dead only a matter of months at the time of Augustine's arrival. The death of a king inevitably introduced a significant degree of political instability, sometimes sparking the outbreak of conflict between as well as within kingdoms. Externally, a serious threat emerged from Brunhild's long-standing rival Fredegund and her son Chlothar II.

Taking advantage of the confusion following Childebert's death, Fredegund and Chlothar occupied Paris, nominally neutral territory since the death of Guntram, making it their royal city instead of Soissons the traditional capital of the Kingdom of Neustria. This was a significant turning point in Frankish history. By 613, Chlothar II would be the only king left in Francia, and the capital city of a single Frankish kingdom was Paris.

In the midst of these events, the arrival of Augustine in the autumn of 596 gave Brunhild what must have seemed an act of providence to strengthen her position in the Austrasian court and at the same time weaken the position of her rivals. Gregory evidently knew enough about Brunhild and her circumstances to expect that her political ambitions would ensure her support for Augustine. The pope's calculations proved correct. The queen responded energetically to Gregory's appeal for support; so much so that Gregory believed Brunhild had contributed more to the success of the mission 'than anyone except God'.[8]

Augustine found himself in a complex power play at the heart of the Austrasian–Burgundian court. Faileuba, Childebert's widow and the mother of the two royal minors, could potentially take control of the regency by mobilizing support from within the Austrasian court. The main source of support that Faileuba needed was from Warnacher, the mayor or *comes* of the palace. Before Brunhild received Augustine, he would first have met with Warnacher who, 17 years later, would betray the queen into the hands of her nephew Chlothar II.

Augustine's arrival served to strengthen Brunhild's position in a number of ways. By providing support for Pope Gregory's mission Brunhild at one stroke would show her piety in backing the venture and simultaneously strengthen her position and prestige at the Austrasian royal court. As Queen Bertha's aunt (by marriage to Sigibert I), Brunhild would also expect to strengthen Austrasian influence over England and in this way further consolidate her power and strengthen her position.

In practical terms, by 596 the Frankish hegemony over Kent had largely dissolved, as none of Chlothar's successors had a clear mandate for oversight of developments with England. This may also account in part for the lack of response to Bertha's pleas for a mission to Kent from the Frankish Church. For Brunhild, however, there was an important political reason to support Augustine's mission. If England belonged not to a vague, Frankish hegemony, but to a specifically Austrasian and Burgundian dominion, then Chlothar II and his kingdom of Neustria would be further marginalized in international Frankish politics.

'The Priests Who Are in Their Neighbourhood'

Gregory's letter to Queen Brunhild carried by Augustine contained two vital pieces of information in regard to the mission: that the Kentish royal household itself had requested the mission and that their initial request to a neighbouring Frankish diocese had gone unheeded:

> we inform you that it has come to our knowledge how that the nation of the Angli, by God's permission, is desirous of becoming Christian, but that the priests who are in their neighbourhood have no pastoral solicitude with regard to them. And lest their souls should haply perish in eternal damnation, it has been our care to send to them the bearer of these presents, Augustine the servant of God, whose zeal and earnestness are well known to us, with other servants

of God; that through them we might be able to learn their wishes, and, as far as is possible, you also striving with us, to take thought for their conversion. We have also charged them that for carrying out this design they should take with them presbyters from the neighbouring regions.[9]

We have considered the issues surrounding who requested the mission; but to whom was the request addressed? And who were the neighbouring clergy who failed to respond? Marilyn Dunn suggests that Childebert, who had died in early 596, may have been the person instrumental in encouraging Pope Gregory to take a more active interest in the conversion of the Anglo-Saxon peoples – particularly those in Kent.[10]

Dunn's argument is that Bertha was beholden to King Chilperic and Neustria for her own Frankish loyalties. Set against this interpretation is Ian Wood's delineation of the Merovingian kingdoms after 561. Charibert's kingdom was extensive, in land-area the largest of the four kingdoms, stretching from the River Canche south of Boulogne to the Pyrenees. Tours, where Charibert's Queen Ingoberga and her daughter Bertha were exiled, also fell within Charibert's domain. Not only was Chilperic's kingdom the smallest before 567, it was also confined to the territory around Soissons near Paris and Toulouse in southwest Francia.

The sharing-out of Charibert's kingdom among the three surviving brothers considerably increased the size of Chilperic's and Sigibert's kingdoms. Guntram of Burgundy was also a beneficiary, receiving fresh territory north of the Loire and also north of Bordeaux. Chilperic now held additional land between the River Canche, the Loire and the sea, but Tours came under the rule of Sigibert of Austrasia. Paris fell to Guntram but was declared part of neutral or shared territory after his death.[11] The new arrangements created a patchwork of territories that were impossible to consolidate within a single border for each of the three kingdoms.

It was during this period of consolidation into the three kingdoms that the city of Tours and its inhabitants, both royal and common, became subjects of Austrasia. This included Bertha, who while living in Tours was given in marriage to Aethelberht. The implication is that Sigibert and not Chilperic would have held the responsibility for Bertha's marriage arrangements, in this way extending Austrasian hegemony over Kent. This state of affairs also makes sense of Gregory's earlier correspondence with Childebert and now in 596 to Brunhild and her grandsons, asking for support for the mission.

Bertha, far from being surprised, annoyed or disappointed at the arrival of Augustine and a Frankish contingent supplied by the Austrasian kingdom, would rather have welcomed their arrival, as subsequent events indicate. Which diocese in northern Francia had failed to heed Bertha's call for a mission? The closest diocese to Kent was Arras (possibly subject to Reims in this period), followed next by Amiens, and both might be expected to fall under the influence of Fredegund and her Neustrian court.

Given the lack of Frankish response over the previous decades, why should Austrasia or Burgundy offer any assistance now, if not because internal Frankish politics made involvement in Kent suddenly a very attractive proposition? It is clear from Gregory's letter to Brunhild that the Frankish Church had not responded to earlier English requests for a mission. Brunhild possessed wolverine acuity in sensing the wind. She championed Augustine's mission for a clear political motive, and it is questionable whether she would have involved herself to any great extent had the political circumstances not made involvement in Kent so attractive.

Gregory's letter contains no specific mention of the support that Augustine would need, nor was he clear concerning which 'neighbouring regions' he had in mind; the pope left such details to his chosen servant for the mission. What Augustine specifically requested is not known, but his negotiations were astute and the support he did receive was, in the end, sufficient to bring the entire mission party safely to the shores of Kent.

Autun *(Augustodonum)* to the River Loire

With the support that Augustine needed now finally secured from Queen Brunhild, the party left the Saône behind and continued overland to the city of Autun and to Syagrius, the bishop most closely linked to Brunhild's royal court. Autun was the logical next stop on a journey from Chalon to Tours. Autun was very much a Roman city, its name an abbreviation of Augustus and once the capital of the ancient druidic *Aedui*. Here Augustus established his new town Augustodonum. It was also the religious centre and melting pot of Celtic, Roman and Eastern cultures. Julius Caesar described the area as the sister and rival of Rome itself.

Brunhild founded a hostel for pilgrims in Autun and also secured papal privileges from Gregory I for her own foundations, including a nunnery founded by Syagrius in Autun in 602. The city was also Brunhild's last resting place. After her death in Amiens in 613, her ashes were brought to the abbey at Autun, dedicated to Saint Martin. As regent Brunhild had asked the pope to grant the pallium to Syagrius. Whether Augustine brought this with him or whether Syagrius received the pallium at a later date is uncertain. This episode was unusual because the pallium was a papal gift reserved for metropolitan bishops, but Autun was not a metropolitan see. Then again, Gregory subsequently refused the pallium to Desiderius, the Metropolitan of Vienne, possibly because of his concerns over the bishop's teaching.

Church and State

The close relationship between Brunhild and Syagrius raises a question whether such relationships were healthy for the mission of the Church, a question that Augustine would also need to answer in Canterbury. The power relationships between a king and his noblemen were complex, and, because the stakes were high, they were also frequently fatal. The fate of those described in Gregory of Tours's *Historiae* as patricians, dukes, counts, mayors, governors and masters of the stables from the time of Clovis's death, reveals just how frequently high-ranking men met a violent end. Possibly one in three Merovingian nobles could expect to die in this way, and the victims of feuds among the powerful were four or five times more numerous than those dying on the battlefield.[12]

Alongside the structures of secular power there were other types of authority principally associated with the Frankish Church. In the Merovingian period Church and State were not easily separable. Ecclesiastical authority, particularly the bishops', was connected to the power of the king through a system of patronage, especially in the urban centres of the Frankish kingdoms. Like Gallo-Roman cities, dioceses were also organized into provinces, their bishops subordinated to a metropolitan overseeing and consecrating the bishops within each secular province. A king also held the power to forbid a bishop to attend a council called by his metropolitan.[13]

Brunhild was hostile to clerics who criticized her regime and active in the appointment of bishops of her own choice, including Gregory of Tours. Domnulus, who replaced Desiderius at Vienne, was almost certainly her appointee. On the other hand, Chilperic, King of Neustria who died in 584, had once complained that no one had any respect for royal authority, all power having passed to the bishops. However, the invocation of divine favour for armies about to engage in war was a matter of crucial importance, and the support of bishops was expected to ensure that such favour accompanied the king's warriors into battle. Christian liturgies came to feature prayers for the victory of the army and the prayers especially hoped for triumph over 'pagans' and 'barbarians'.

Many bishops of the late Roman period had been notable civil servants or soldiers earlier in their secular careers – in the mould of Ambrose of Milan and Martin of Tours. They were often well placed to run the temporal aspects of their sees. Others had been *comes*, chief officials or mayors of the palace, before consecration as bishop. In many respects the Frankish bishops were comparable to secular magnates (ultra-wealthy aristocrats) and for the most part were drawn from the same aristocratic class.

Just as the king needed the support of his magnates, so he needed the support of his bishops. Similarly, as most magnates needed royal patronage in terms of lands and office, so did the leading clergy of the kingdom. The Frankish Church had a decided advantage in that the bishops controlled significant wealth that, unlike private fortunes, could not be dissipated through inheritance or dowries.

Royal involvement in episcopal appointments suggests that the kings and their bishops were, with a few notable exceptions, likely to work together rather than in opposition. As the bishops became more powerful figures in local politics, service in the Church provided an alternative route to directly serving the king, so gaining access to the royal presence. Bishops at times played a crucial role in the factional politics of the period. It is not surprising, however, that the pope regarded the Frankish Church as stained with simony, and in turning to Brunhild to help reform these abuses, Gregory I was appealing to the person most implicated in determining episcopal appointments.

As a Catholic, Brunhild was subject to the authority of the pope, and Gregory seems to have had little regard for the views of Frankish secular rulers when it came to Augustine's consecration in Arles. This was in striking contrast to the way that Church–State relations usually operated in Francia. As pope and head of the Catholic Church, Gregory may not even have considered requesting Brunhild's permission for an ecclesiastical decision. Bishop Etherius of Lyon, whose own appointment had relied on Brunhild's support, might have been relieved not to be directly involved in Augustine's consecration in the event that she might have disapproved.

The 'distinctive vocation of the classical city' had no place in Merovingian royal households that revelled in private pursuits on their country estates, and withdrew behind the walls of former Roman cities, sometimes uneasily sharing public space with a bishop and cathedral. However, the Frankish Church, placing a high value on hierarchical obedience and vying for power and influence on more equal terms with secular rulers, also had little interest in the notion of public citizenship. How distinctively different this might have been in comparison to Gregory's Rome is difficult to assess; however, the master class in Church–State relations that a journey through the Frankish kingdoms gave to Augustine was invaluable in his later dealings with Bertha and Aethelberht in Canterbury.

Notes

1 Norman Davies, *Vanished Kingdoms: The History of Half-Forgotten Europe*, Harmondsworth: Penguin (iBook), 2011, p. 103.
2 Gregory the Great, Book VI, Letter 54.
3 David Abulafia, *The Great Sea: A Human History of the Mediterranean*, London: Allen Lane (Penguin) (iBook), 2011, p. 248.
4 Peter Heather, *Empires and Barbarians: Migration, Development and the Birth of Europe*, Oxford: Pan Books, 2009, p. 313.
5 Alain Dierkens and Patrick Perin, 'Les sedes regiae mérovingiennes entre Seine et Rhin', in Gisela Ripoll and Josep Gurt (eds), *Sedes regiae (ann. 400–800)*, Barcelona: Reial Acadèmia de Bones Lletres, 2000, p. 288.
6 Jean-Denis G. G. Lepage, *Castles and Fortified Cities of Medieval Europe: An Illustrated History*, London: McFarland & Company, 2001.
7 Daniel G. Russo, *Town Origins and Development in Early England, c.400–950 A.D.*, Westport and London: Greenwood Publishing Group, 1998, p. 170.
8 Gregory the Great, Book XI, Letter 48.
9 Gregory the Great, Book VI, Letter 59; see also Ian Wood, 'Augustine and Gaul', in R. Gameson (ed.), *St Augustine and the Conversion of England*, Stroud: Sutton Publishing Ltd, 1999, p. 68.
10 Marilyn Dunn, *The Christianization of the Anglo-Saxons c. 597–c. 700: Discourses of Life, Death and Afterlife*, London: Continuum, 2009, p. 49.
11 Ian Wood, *The Merovingian Kingdoms, 450–751*, London and New York: Longman, 1994, pp. 368–9.
12 Ross Samson, 'The Merovingian nobleman's home: Castle or villa?', *Journal of Medieval History* 13:4 (1987), p. 288.
13 Wood, *Merovingian Kingdoms*, p. 71.

6

The Loire to Tours

As Augustine's journey continued from the colder hill country of Autun down to the more temperate riverside town of Nevers (a drop of nearly 2000 feet), there was much to digest from his recent encounter with Queen Brunhild. Some implications for the future would be hard to foresee, and the absence of any letter from Gregory to the Neustrian King Chlothar II or his bishops could yet prove a weakness in Gregory's plan. But for the moment, he had the support of the queen and her authority to command the resources that he needed. Syagrius, Bishop of Autun, arranged for Augustine's onward journey to Nevers and the Loire, a distance by road of 53 miles (85 km), which in turn would take the missionaries downstream to Orléans and finally to Tours.

For several centuries before Augustine's arrival the Loire had already become one of the great highways of ancient Gaul. The Loire was more than a means of transport or a resource for agriculture; it also represented a cultural and political divide between North and South. The Loire is the longest river in France, extending for over 1000 kilometres. Its source lies in the *Massif Centrale*, from which it flows northwards through Roanne and Nevers to Orléans, then continues westward through Tours to Nantes, where it finally opens into a broad estuary.

The river comprises three definable segments: the Upper Loire, which is an area from the source to its confluence with the Allier; the Middle Loire Valley, a region from the Allier to its confluence with the River Maine below Tours, a distance of about 280 km (170 miles); and finally the Lower Loire, from the Maine to the estuary and the Atlantic Ocean. Phoenicians and Greeks, travelling from the Mediterranean basin to the Atlantic coast, had used packhorses to transport goods from Lyon to the Loire. The Romans used barges on the Loire at Roanne to within 93 miles of its source, and two centuries after Augustine Viking long boats entered the Loire from the sea and pillaged as far inland as the city of Tours. The Norsemen would do the same to Canterbury.

The Loire is sometimes called 'the last wild river in Europe', and springtime floods alternate with dry summers and very low water levels. The river flow is particularly strong in the Upper Loire from Roanne, once a Roman port, to the confluence with the River Allier at Nevers. From Nevers, river navigation would become easier for Augustine, leaving the narrow gorges and turbulent waters of the Upper Loire behind. In the central section of the Loire Valley the approach to Orléans is made difficult through numerous sand banks and islands. The seasons largely determine the water flow, and from August to September the river turns sluggish from Orléans to the sea. The Loire usually floods in February and March. With such variability in water levels and the current, the use of the Loire for navigation has always been very limited, particularly for barges with a draft greater than 120–140 cm.

What this meant for Augustine, probably arriving at Nevers in November, was that he could expect the outward journey to Tours to be slow as autumn drew on. However, to have a realistic chance of arriving in England before Easter (which in 597 fell in late April), it would be essential to leave Tours by the end of January or the beginning of February at the latest. The final leg of their journey would begin in the dead of winter and at the worst time of the year. The missionaries faced the possibility of floods and raging torrents, which would force the party to take a slower route north by road. There were few other viable options, because the Loire 'was the main highway until well into the nineteenth century, the most useful and comfortable way to travel. Roads were awful. Coaches were sprung only with leather straps and horses pulling carts could manage only about five to eight kilometres a day.'[1] Further downstream, a typical journey by barge from Orléans to Nantes might take eight days, while a return journey upstream against a strong flow could increase the time to 14 days.

Winter Food Supplies and the Cycle of the Seasons

The Loire's temperate maritime climate produces warmer winters and fewer extremes in temperature, making the region one of the most agreeable areas of northern France. Despite this, food supplies for the missionaries' journey were not plentiful. In the rural areas of Francia, from before the sixth century until the early twentieth, 99 per cent of all agricultural activity took place between late spring and early autumn. The agricultural year consisted of two seasons – 'seven months of winter [November to May], and five months of hell [June to October]'.[2] This meant that during the winter months human hibernation for most people was a physical and economic necessity: lowering the body's metabolic rate prevented hunger that would arise as winter supplies and human bodies became exhausted. Further west on the Loire, in troglodyte cave-villages between Tours and Angers, subsistence farmers did not stir during winter, and even the more temperate regions on Augustine's route such as the Central Loire retreated into idleness during the winter months.

As autumn turned to winter Augustine's ability to obtain food supplies for his companions would become increasingly difficult. In rural places such as these, far away from towns and cities, there would be no surpluses to share and almost no one from whom to purchase supplies.

The ancient Roman feast of *Saturnalia*, honouring the god Saturn, was still widely celebrated as a weeklong festival in December. The feast included observance of the winter solstice on 21 December, the shortest day of the year, when the sun seems to stand still before slowly turning towards the new life of spring. The winter solstice celebration was crucial for communities that had no certainty of surviving the winter.

Starvation was common in 'the famine months' between January and April. In a temperate climate such as the Lower Loire, the midwinter festival was the last feast before deep winter began. Cattle were slaughtered so they would not have to be fed during the winter, and this was almost the only time of year when a supply of fresh meat was available and wine was in abundant supply. This would prove immensely important to Augustine in selecting a time for the first large scale baptism of Saxon converts one year later in Kent.

Saint Martin's Year

The influence of the cycle of the seasons was clearly evident in Martin's pastoral ministry and those who followed him, including Gregory of Tours. A bishop's summer could be spent on long journeys to attend the king at his royal court, meet with his metropolitan and attend a synod, tend to the affairs of the Church far from his episcopal city or lead missionary efforts to rural areas where Celtic, pagan or Druidic communities still overwhelmingly predominated.

By September Martin would be back in his see city for a short period until the winter round of visiting began once more. Mid-November until the end of December would usually be spent visiting and preaching the gospel around his diocese, travelling sometimes by boat, on foot or on mule. The weather until Epiphany (6 January) was not usually exceptionally cold in the Central Loire region, and devotees of ancient pagan gods gathered to celebrate at numerous shrines in the rural hinterland.

From January the Loire could be in full spate and most of the roads impassable. During this time Martin would withdraw to Tours through the remainder of winter, preparing to keep the fast of Lent in spring. It is also the time that Augustine would need to leave Tours for the final leg of the journey to Canterbury.

In 596 the city of Orléans was the former capital of Burgundy and somewhat diminished in status after the royal court moved to Chalon. This was also true of Metz, as both their young kings now lived in Chalon, with the dowager queen. However, there would still be an administrative and military presence in the city, and it would be to this group that Augustine now turned in securing supplies and barges for his onward journey to Tours. This meant flat-bottomed boats with large but fold-able masts, able to gather wind from above the riverbanks, but which also allowed easy passage under bridges. At Orléans a submerged dike once divided the river into north- and south-flowing watercourses; the latter carried Augustine and his Roman missionaries to Tours.

A journey on the Loire of less than a week from Orléans would bring Augustine to Tours. The route carried him past Amboise where Saint Martin had established one of five monasteries as missionary outposts to pagans, whom he called the 'country-dwelling people'. Martin's Marmoutier Abbey (*monasterium maiorum*, the great monastery), some four kilometres east of Tours, would be clearly visible to Augustine's party from the river. In the city itself, Saint Gatien's Cathedral and Saint Martin's Basilica lay on an east–west axis from the cathedral in the east to Saint Martin's Basilica to the west. The shrine was outside the city wall and supported by its own monastic community.

Augustine at Tours (*Caesarodonum*)

Caesarodonum was built as a Roman *castrum* in the year AD 1. By the end of the sixth century Tours had become both spiritually and politically significant, owing substantially to the cult-centre of Saint Martin, who was widely recognized as a miracle-working saint by both the Roman and Irish Churches. During his lifetime (316–97) and particularly in his role as bishop, Martin had gained a reputation as an innovator in his approach to converting rural areas to Christ. Since miracle-working was a *sine qua non* for missionaries, Martin provided a model for Augustine as he prepared for his own mission in Kent.

There were compelling reasons for Augustine's significant detour to reach Tours so late in the year. While there is no definitive evidence that Bertha was in fact a resident of Tours before her marriage to Aethelberht of Kent, she nevertheless had close connections with Tours and chose Martin as the patron saint of her own chapel in Canterbury. It is possible that Bertha may have lived in Le Mans, as did her mother Ingoberga, but no chapel or church there was dedicated to Saint Martin, and the city's cathedral was dedicated to Saint Julian.

Although hardly on the most direct route to England, a visit to Tours could have seemed spiritually as well as politically important. It was the cult centre of St Martin (d. 397), a pioneer of monasticism, a bishop who had been concerned for the conversion of rural Gaul, and an enormously popular miracle-working saint. In addition, Bertha, the Frankish queen of Kent, had close family connections with Tours: it was within the kingdom that had been ruled, albeit briefly, by her father, King Charibert (561–7); more significantly, her mother, Ingoberga, had been a friend of Bishop Gregory of Tours (d. 594) and a benefactor to two churches there; while her sister, Berthefled, had been a nun in the town. It may thus have seemed a likely source of information about Kent, and a potential way of ensuring a favourable reception there.[3]

There may have been an additional reason for Augustine's detour. Seven years earlier (in 589) Agiulf, one of Gregory of Tours's deacons, had travelled to Rome to receive some relics of Saint Martin and stayed on to witness Gregory the Great's papal election. It seems highly likely that Agiulf met Augustine in Rome during this time, and Agiulf may have arranged hospitality for Augustine and his companions during their stay in Tours. He may also have helped in selecting Frankish priests who would be good interpreters and preachers for the mission in Canterbury. All in all, the city was the most likely source of recent information about events in Kent.

One of Bede's few references to the journey through Francia records that Gregory the Great instructed Augustine to find translators, so that his Latin-speaking missionaries could preach to the Anglo-Saxons.[4] Tours was the most likely and also the last place from which to draw interpreters who were priests knowledgeable in the Scriptures and who knew how to preach. Queen Brunhild had given her full backing to this, and the Frankish addition to the mission would have included not only priests but also clerks in minor orders, perhaps drawn from both the cathedral and Saint Martin's Abbey. They later received particular mention in Augustine's letter from Canterbury to Gregory.[5] The addition of Frankish interpreters to Augustine's party would have been one significant reason for Gregory's comment that the mission owed more to Brunhild than to anyone else, except God.

While in Tours, Augustine would also have prayed at Saint Martin's shrine and learned what he could of Martin's ministry. A copy of Sulpicius Severus's early *Life of Saint Martin* would have been held at Saint Martin's Abbey. Tours was also to be an excellent location from which to learn more of the Merovingian dynasty. Gregory of Tours had died only two years earlier; his ten-volume *Historia Francorum* would have been in the hands of Pelagius, his successor as bishop at Saint Gatien's Cathedral, and this too would have been available to Augustine.

Martin's Life and Influence

Martin was born at Sabaria, a notable frontier garrison town in Pannonia (present-day Szombathely in Hungary). He grew up in Milan (*Mediolanum*) where as a catechumen at the age of ten he prepared for baptism. However, before Martin was able to receive baptism, he was forcefully conscripted into the Roman cavalry and at the age of 18 was stationed at Amiens (*Samarobriva*) in northwestern Gaul. Here the young cavalry officer had a life-transforming experience when he encountered a poorly clothed beggar freezing in the cold at the gates of the city. Martin is said to have cut his own cavalry cloak in two, giving half to the beggar. That night Martin dreamt of Christ, wearing the half-cloak that he had given away. He heard the Lord say to the angels, 'Here is Martin, the Roman soldier who is not baptized; he has clad me.'[6] Another version of the story describes that when Martin awoke, he found that his cloak had been fully restored. Now a Christian, Martin resigned his commission as a soldier, but with considerable opposition from his superiors.

In the life of Martin on the one hand, and the life of the recently deceased Gregory of Tours on the other, Augustine had two very different models of episcopal leadership to reflect upon. Martin had established a monastery, Leguge, in Poitiers, then another at Indre-et-Loire and finally another at Marmoutier near Tours. Martin as a 'missionary bishop' was particularly active in the rural areas to the west of Tours two centuries before Augustine's mission to Canterbury.

The burdens of being a city-based bishop proved overwhelming for Martin as streams of people came to him for a private audience concerning both local and wider issues, such as the bureaucracy of the Church and the administration of properties and plate. In search of a place in which to find peace and solitude, Martin crossed the Loire and came to an open meadow that lay between the river and chalk cliffs dotted with caves. Here Martin built a wooden hut and adopted the lifestyle and garb of a hermit. A different group was now drawn to Martin, and they came for a very different reason: to seek training in the spiritual life. A monastery soon followed, and a monastic house for women was opened in Tours. It is likely that Bertha's sister was a latter-day member of this community.

In fourth-century Gaul, Christians had largely been confined to urban areas, where most bishops and priests were to be found. However, Martin did not attempt to convert rural pagans from a distance. His approach was to visit a remote region and travel from house to house speaking to people about God, much as Bede describes Saint Aidan's activities in seventh-century Northumbria. Martin organized converts into a community under the direction of a priest or monk. To encourage them in their faith, he would visit these new communities at least once a year. Martin was one of the first bishops to insist on visiting each of his parishes every year, no matter how remote. This rudimentary parochial system became the key to establishing and maintaining the faith of newly converted rural Christians. Actions such as these would have been important to Augustine as he began to formulate an effective strategy for mission in a culture very different from his own.

Although Martin is the patron saint of France and his principal shrine is at Tours, he is also important to Irish and British monastic traditions. Martin was one of the foremost pioneers of Western monasticism before Benedict, directly influencing many of the monasteries established in Ireland and Scotland. Irish and Welsh missionaries revered Saint Martin, and his monastery at Marmoutier became the training ground for many Irish missions. Patrick is said to be one of many notables who lived for a time at the Abbey of Marmoutier. Ninian (d. 432) had studied at Marmoutier and was profoundly influenced by Martin, carrying his ministry back to Scotland. Ninian dedicated his church to Martin, beginning a long history of dedications to the saint, including the oldest surviving English church, Saint Martin's in Canterbury.

Martin's ministry was, at heart, that of pastor and healer. He had for some years studied the lives and methods of the desert prophets, Elijah and Elisha. The miraculous ministry of Jesus seemed, to Martin, to show people unambiguously that the Kingdom of God was come upon them. Martin also possessed a working knowledge of the human body through practical first-aid as a field soldier, and he was able to discern when moral encouragement or spiritual healing was called for. A ministry among the sick was also a challenge to the work of Satan in bringing death, disease and suffering into the human condition. In this, Martin identified himself with the mind of the Early Church and drew his lay community of Marmoutier and the Cathedral of Saint-Gatien in Tours to share in his ministry. This served to make the Christian message and Christian life enormously appealing.

Augustine also features in a miracle story associated with the region of Anjou. According to a French tradition, Augustine and his companions arrived weary and tired at Ponts-de-Cé on the Lower Loire. They had scarcely crossed the river when a rough crowd from Cé began to assault the missionaries. At this, Augustine took up his staff to ward off the blows. However, God intervened: the saint's arm stretched out like a bow, and his staff shot some 300 yards as though fired like an arrow. Where it struck the ground a spring gushed out, and the astonished crowd ended their attack. That night supernatural lights were said to have rested over the elm tree where the missionaries slept.[7]

It is possible that this story confuses Augustine with Martin who, after settling a local dispute in Anjou, fell ill and died there shortly afterwards. Nevertheless, this miracle story suggests that the first Bishop of Canterbury left the city and went out and about among the rural people in difficult circumstances and in distant heathen places, as Martin had done two centuries before. It may also indicate the moment that Augustine found himself exercising his missionary ministry in a new way, beginning from the moment that he stepped on to the shores of Kent.

In contrast to Martin the missionary, Gregory the historian, who had served as Bishop of Tours for 21 years in 573–94, was a member of the wealthy senatorial class from which most Roman–Gallic bishops were then drawn. His life was one of almost ceaseless activity, at ease with being in constant demand, comfortable to be in charge of a church bureaucracy, an organizer and church-builder, an able administrator of church property and plate and a frequent entertainer of key figures, both local and international. Gregory settled disputes, was often found at the royal court as an adviser, disputed against heretics and found time to write a history of the Franks.

Gregory of Tours lived in a very different Francia from the Gaul that Martin had known; Merovingian Francia was wealthier and more sophisticated, more overtly Christian, but also more corrupt and steeped in an all-pervasive culture of violence.

Saint Martin's Shrine at Tours

Martin's popularity arose in part from his adoption as a saintly mascot by successive royal houses of the Merovingian dynasty. In 507 Clovis, on the way to battle near Poitiers against Alaric II of the Arian Goths, sent messengers to Saint Martin's shrine to ask for an oracle concerning the outcome of the battle. The monks were chanting words from a Psalm, 'For Thou hast girded me with strength unto the battle; Thou hast subdued under me those that rose up against me . . .', as the messengers entered the chapel. Clovis took this as a sign and later returned to Tours as victor of the battle.

From that time crowds flocked to Saint Martin's shrine from all over Francia. The Abbey of Marmoutier, which during Martin's lifetime had lived by faith as it scrimped and fasted its way in prayer and contemplation, suddenly became the wealthiest monastery in the country as gifts were showered upon it by rich and poor alike. Similarly, the Abbey of Saint-Martin at Tours became one of the most prominent and influential establishments in medieval Francia. Within its chapel a large block of marble above the tomb of Saint Martin made the shrine visible to the faithful gathered behind the high altar and also to pilgrims encamped in the atrium of the basilica.

The numinous power that attached to the saint's body was widely attested by providing oracles for kings before battle, healing the sick, settling family disputes, discerning which oaths were true and which false, defending the city and providing sanctuary from the long arm of the king. However, beneath it all lay its main purpose, from the Church's perspective: to enhance ecclesiastical power and buttress the authority of the Bishop of Tours and his clergy. This could scarcely have escaped Augustine's notice as a monk sent to England, because the pope could not entrust the task to his own Roman bishops who, even in these 'last days', were caught up in a vortex of ecclesiastical positioning and power politics.

Saint Martin's cloak, preserved at Marmoutier Abbey for over 100 years after Martin's death, had already become a significant relic. After Clovis's victory over Alaric II the cloak was kept as their symbol of legitimacy as well as the private possession of the Merovingian kings. They took the cloak everywhere, even into battle. The priests who cared for and carried Saint Martin's cloak were called *cappellani*. The French translation for this is *chapelains*, from which the English word 'chaplain' derives. Because of the significance of the cloak, Merovingian support for the cult of Saint Martin, beginning with Clovis I, was enormously important for both the status and the wealth of the city of Tours.

In contrast to this, the symbol of Saint Martin's simple eremitic life and pastoral ministry was a three-legged wooden stool, such as those found in milking sheds across the country. Martin took his stool everywhere he travelled, eschewing the episcopal throne and Constantinian power that came with it.

All this may have passed through Augustine's mind as he prayed at Saint Martin's shrine, now a far more impressive basilica than the first wooden structure hastily erected by Bricius, Martin's ambitious disciple and successor. As Augustine prayed, would he choose the rough milking stool or embrace the warm chaplain's cloak as the hallmark of his own episcopacy in Canterbury?

Bertha and the Influence of Martin

Bertha would have been familiar with the monastic life and the positive impact Christianity had made on the lives of the Frankish people. Both of Bertha's younger sisters were nuns: Bertilflede in Tours itself and the youngest, Theologilda, at Sainte-Croix in Poitiers. Bertha seems to have known Gregory of Tours, who was consecrated bishop in c. 573. Gregory mentions Ingoberga and her daughter Bertha's marriage in his writings and may have been instrumental in its arrangement, together with her uncle Guntram and possibly even Queen Brunhild, who was Bertha's aunt by marriage.

Less clear is what aspect of the life of Saint Martin Bertha carried with her to Canterbury, when she dedicated her royal chapel to his name. Was it his life and ministry of healing and pastoral care for the poor? Or, as a Merovingian princess, would she have in mind her family's royal cult of Saint Martin and his cloak, the trappings and reinforcement of Merovingian power? How Augustine was able both to conceive and carry out the mission among the *Angli* would depend very much on the answer.

The Road from Tours

The trail runs cold once Augustine and his party, now 40 in number, leave Tours. None of Gregory's surviving letters were written to bishops or royal figures north of the Loire or Saône, so that the route Augustine followed remains the subject of speculation; however, the choices open to him are clear enough. Would he travel north to reach the coast at Quentovic through the Neustrian Kingdom and Paris? Or would he attempt the much longer journey northeast through Reims, which would enable the missionaries to remain under Queen Brunhild's protection?

As the missionaries left the city of Tours behind, Augustine may have followed the ancient practice of many pilgrims in earlier centuries and travelled from one abbey and church to another that was dedicated to Saint Martin, throwing himself upon divine protection rather than Merovingian assurances to bring him safely to the coast.

Notes

1 Christopher Donaldson, *The Great English Pilgrimage: From Rome to Canterbury*, Norwich: Canterbury Press, 1995, p. 89.
2 Graham Robb, *The Discovery of France: A Historical Geography*, New York: W. W. Norton & Co., 2007, p. 75.

3 Richard Gameson, *St Augustine and the Conversion of England*, Stroud: Sutton Publishing Ltd, 1999, p. 12.
4 Bede, *Ecclesiastical History* I.25.
5 Bede, *Ecclesiastical History* I.27; Augustine's first question.
6 Alexander Roberts, 'Sulpitius Severus on the Life of St Martin', in P. Schaff and H. Wace (eds), *A Select Library of Nicene and Post-Nicene Fathers of the Christian Church*, 2nd series, Vol. 1, Oxford: James Parker & Company, 1984, Ch. 2.
7 G. H. Doble, *Saint Augustine of Canterbury in Anjou*, Truro: Netherton and Worth, 1932, p. 38.

7

Paris (*Lutetia Parisiorum*) to Quentovic

Travelling from Tours with nearly 40 people, including baggage, wagons, mules and supplies and possibly an armed guard furnished by Brunhild, the final stage would take Augustine north to the emporium port of Quentovic. The shortest route passed through Neustrian territory by way of Paris and Amiens to Quentovic, a distance of about 290 miles.

From the distribution of Gregory's letters to Francia in 596, the pope initially chose to ignore the young King Chlothar II, and more significantly his mother Fredegund, as partners in the mission. Gregory's *Regesta* for that year contains no letters written to either, nor to any of the bishops in the kingdom of Neustria. The absence of any letters to the Neustrian bishops would seem to confirm that Gregory chose to avoid contact with Neustria, perhaps aware that little support would be forthcoming from Queen Fredegund, by this stage either dead or an ailing dowager.

Nevertheless, in 601 Gregory wrote to Chlothar II praising his support for Augustine's mission, indicating that some contact was made and support given in 597. 'Now certain monks [Laurentius and Peter], who had proceeded with our most reverend brother and fellow bishop Augustine to the nation of the Angli, have returned and told us with what great charity your Excellence refreshed this our brother when he was present with you, and with what supports you aided him on his departure.'[1]

Had there been no substance to this Gregory would scarcely have made such a blatantly false attempt to flatter Chlothar for his non-existent support; particularly as by 601, Chlothar was still 11 years away from his accession to the rulership of the whole Merovingian kingdom and his future prospects were far from certain, while Brunhild still exercised considerable power in Francia.

Gregory's letter to Chlothar is the only evidence for the route Augustine might have followed to reach the English Channel and suggests that the missionaries did pass through Neustrian territory. A possible scenario is that Augustine's journey to Tours, far west on the Loire, favoured the shortest route north, through Neustria. Pope Gregory's letter to Chlothar II in 601 strongly indicates that the king provided some form of aid to Augustine and granted permission to cross his domain with a large party, half of whom were from a rival kingdom.

Arrival in Paris *(Lutetia)*

Paris occupies a natural limestone basin hollowed out by the Seine that winds northwest towards the Normandy coast about 93 miles (150 km) downstream. Germanic invasions by the Franks and Alemanni in the late third century destroyed many of the Left Bank buildings in this Gallo-Roman city. Paris was forced to contract into the defensive stronghold of Île de la Cité using the Seine as a protective barrier. Walls were built along the island perimeter using large stones dragged from ruins on the Left Bank.

There were many sides to Paris.

The city was deeply rooted in legend and superstition. The edges of the city, both north and south of the Seine, had been left to decay over succeeding centuries following the Roman withdrawal and slowly sank into the surrounding countryside. In tune with the spiritual climate of Paris at the time, werewolves as well as packs of dogs were believed to inhabit everyday life. On Île de la Cité, the historic heart of ancient Paris, a pagan altar lay buried beneath the public square that now stands before the Cathedral of Our Lady of Paris. An earlier Gallo-Roman temple stood beneath the cathedral itself, and this had replaced an even earlier shrine sacred to the ancient gods of Lutetia.

A legend connects Paris with sub-Roman Britain. Here in 464 Arthur, the son of Uther Pendragon, is said to have called upon the Virgin Mary for protection in his forthcoming battle near Paris with a Roman military detachment. The Virgin offered Arthur her cloak, and the hero of British legend was able to defeat Flolo, the Roman tribune.[2]

Paris was a city deeply rooted in religious conviction. Saint Geneviève built a prominent shrine to Saint Denis (Dionysius, d. 250), the first missionary martyr of ancient Lutetia. The church was built on an ancient Roman road that crossed Île de la Cité and continued some six miles further north to the site of the new church, then continued to Amiens. Saint-Denis was visible to all who passed by as they travelled south to Paris or north to Amiens. A mile or so to the west, the Seine twists and turns back on itself on its long journey towards the sea. The area around Saint-Denis was held to be the sacred centre of Gaul. Julius Caesar recorded that Druids from as far away as Britannia and the Mediterranean came to these Lutetian marshes for the purpose of electing their supreme spiritual leader.

Paris was also deeply layered with symbolism. The city contained both the palace and mausoleum of Clovis, founder of the Merovingian dynasty. After Clovis I converted to Christianity Paris became a significant religious centre. In 556–8, during the reign of Clovis's son Childebert I, the Church of Sainte-Croix-et-Saint-Vincent was built. Chlothar I was buried at Saint-Médard in 561, which he had built and dedicated to the saint in Soissons. Saint Germain, Bishop of Paris and a principal inspiration for the church's dedication, established an adjacent monastery dedicated to Saint Symphorien. In the chapel Childebert placed the tunic of Saint Vincent that had been brought from the Holy Land. The church also preserves Childebert's remains; he died on the day of the church's consecration in 558.

The Prieure Saint-Martin-des-Champs (Saint Martin in the Fields) in Paris was mentioned in a charter dating from 709/10, providing the earliest mention of Saint Martin's Priory in Paris. The priory was located within the city walls on the north bank of the Seine, on the Rue St-Martin, leading to the city gate Porte St-Martin. A religious community may have existed on this site as early as 558. It is possible that Saint Martin's Priory was Augustine's destination in Paris, but to reach it from the south after a long day's journey meant crossing the Seine by way of two over-crowded bridges leading to and from the Île de la Cité.

Further north and outside the city walls of Paris, the basilica of Saint-Denis was the last resting place of Neustrian kings from early times. The remains of Clovis I were not transferred to Saint-Denis (from the crypt of Saint-Geneviève, on the Left Bank of the Seine) until the eighteenth century.

Childebert I (d. 558) was succeeded by his nephew Charibert I, who ruled Paris from 561 until his death in 567. However, Charibert was not buried in Saint-Denis near Paris but in *Blavia Castellum*, a military fort by the sea in the *Tractus Armoricani*, in present-day Normandy. Charibert's daughter Bertha was probably born in the royal palace on Île de la Cité, the city that Chlothar II of Neustria and his mother Fredegund were anxious to seize in 596. The treatment handed out to her father's mortal remains clearly influenced Bertha's own views on dynastic burial in Canterbury.

The Capture of Paris

The taking of Paris was an opportunistic move by Fredegund and Chlothar II, but seizing the city had much deeper significance than simply taking control of its tax revenues. Symbolism was a powerful weapon in the struggle for control of Francia. Fredegund was making a statement about Chlothar's legitimacy, much disputed at the time of his birth, through establishing her son in Francia's ancient dynastic capital.

In 508 the Merovingian King Clovis established his capital in Paris with Queen Clothild. Disaster struck in 586, when Paris was devastated as house after house was set ablaze, 'until the fire came to a small oratory built to commemorate how St Martin had once kissed a leper ... All this devastation must still have been in many people's minds, and the miracle, 11 years later as the pilgrims came in 596–7.'[3] By early 597 Charibert's former royal palace on Île de la Cité had only recently become Chlothar II's own royal seat. The small island, still surrounded by fortified walls, made a defensible area with the Seine serving as a moat. Nevertheless, Paris in 597 might have seemed a rather insignificant, busy little town on an island in the middle of the River Seine.

In early 597 Chlothar II was still a minor, and his mother Fredegund, who had been his chief protector, was on her deathbed. The kingdom of Neustria over which he ruled comprised some lands north of the Loire – a mere 12 cantons between the Seine, the Oise and the sea. It was also the smallest kingdom in Francia. However, in 613 Chlothar II was to become the sole ruler of the Merovingian dynasty, and Paris became the capital of all Franks. A year later Chlothar was sufficiently influential to call a Council at Paris, attended by bishops from throughout Neustria, Austrasia, Burgundy and Aquitaine as well as from Kent – represented by Justus, Bishop of Rochester and Peter, Abbot of Dover. Laurentius was still Archbishop of Canterbury at this time, but did not attend.

The Annual Marchfields Assemblies in 597

In each of the Merovingian kingdoms the political community came together in public assemblies on 1 March, an event known as the Marchfields gathering. Their origin may have been a practice begun by Julius Caesar. In his account of the Gallic Wars, *de Bello Gallico* (c. 50 BC) he refers to Paris as the place where an annual assembly was held between himself as commander of the Roman Legions and local Gallic leaders.

The 1 March assemblies in Francia provided an important and fundamental institutional underpinning for the Merovingian rulers. These Marchfields gatherings brought together church councils, the army muster and the king's court. The chance for Brunhild to strike a blow against her old enemy Fredegund may have provided the motivation behind the 597 declaration of war by Austrasia and Burgundy against Neustria, a decision that would be made at the annual 1 March assembly of the army.

Augustine may have arrived in Paris around the time of the annual Marchfields gathering, particularly if he aimed to reach Canterbury to celebrate Easter in mid-April that year, the most important celebration in the Church's calendar. Had his party taken the route through Austrasia instead, there would have been no celebrations of the Mass at Saint Martin's in Canterbury by Augustine.

Augustine's Departure from Paris

The final part of Augustine's journey most probably took the missionaries northwest from Paris to Beauvais. Here, by tradition, Saint Lucianus, sent to Beauvais by Pope Fabianus, was martyred in the city in c. 275, together with his companions Maxianus and Julianus. From Beauvais, the party would proceed directly to Amiens, on the basin of the Somme, where the rivers Selle, Avre and the Somme meet.

The cult of Saint Martin in fifth-century Gaul and sixth-century Francia was both a vital force in social and political life and a distinctive expression of Christian religion. In the first half of the fifth century his comrades in arms elected Merovech leader in Amiens, and 60 years later Clovis I named his dynasty 'Merovingian' in recognition of this semi-legendary forebear. However, for the later Merovingian dynasty, Amiens was less the city of their founding father Merovech than the city at whose gates Saint Martin divided his cloak with a beggar. Here too, Queen Brunhild met her end, dragged through the streets by an unbroken horse after a show-trial at the hands of her nephew, Chlothar of Paris.

From Amiens the route continued due west on the Somme to Pont-Remy, which lies 26 miles northwest of Amiens, and then to Abbeville.

Quentovic

The final section of the journey seems to have continued to the ancient Frankish port of Quentovic, near present-day Étaples. The distance from Paris to Quentovic via Amiens is approximately 168 miles by road, nearly a month's travel for Augustine's party.

While some of the major seaports of medieval Europe still continue to flourish as ports – such as medieval Hamwic, now the container port of Southampton – others have sunk beneath silted estuaries as trade routes changed over time. Quentovic, a trading post that linked northern Gaul to Britannia, is chief of these lost ports of Europe. The place-name means 'the market on the Canche', a minor river with a large estuary lying some 18 miles (29 km) south of Boulogne.[4] Its more precise location in northern France, after archaeological investigations in the late 1980s, has been identified around the rural hamlet of Visemarest, near Montreuil in the Canche valley, about 8 miles (10 km) inland from the estuary.

The Canche Estuary has served as a hospitable location for various maritime trading centres or *wics* (emporia) from the Bronze Age onwards. The Dover Boat (c. 1550 BC) is one example of a vessel designed for the busy trade routes between the British Isles and trading settlements on the Continent during that period.

At the end of the sixth century Quentovic was an unfortified settlement comprising Frankish, Saxon and Frisian merchants, who were mainly involved in the trade of luxury goods with southern England. Perhaps ranking only after Marseille and Arles, Quentovic was the principal early medieval port in northern Francia and possibly the most important seaport of the Franks, certainly of the northern Frankish homelands. The emerging coastal trading emporia at Dorestad, Ipswich and Quentovic all shared certain characteristics: they formed a loose economic network, with individuals, goods and ideas travelling between them. Dorestad comprised a coastal trading village, harbour and cemetery located in the delta region of the Rhine and Maas and later extensive warehousing. Ipswich had piers, warehouses and shops, but much business would simply be conducted from the holds of boats. Quentovic would have operated on much the same basis.

It is likely that Quentovic was under the control of Neustria and Chlothar II during this period. The Canche seems to have marked the northernmost border of Charibert's former kingdom and later also for Neustria after the division of the Merovingian kingdom (following Charibert's death) in 567.[5]

Augustine's Leadership in Francia

How effective was Augustine's leadership in this initial stage of the mission? Bede's record of the Frankish expedition, from the time that Augustine took his leave for a second time from Gregory the Great to his landing in England, merely states: 'So Augustine, strengthened by the encouragement of St Gregory, in company with the servants of Christ, returned to the work of preaching the word, and came to Britain.'[6] Was there more to it than this?

Augustine adapted the traditional monastic model of Saint Andrew's in Rome, which was intended for a permanent and settled community, into a monastery-on-the-move. He also needed to hold his party together for an extended period of nearly a year and sometimes in tedious, difficult and potentially dangerous circumstances.

What would make the journey tedious would be its length (more than a thousand miles by land, sea and river) and the weather – hot and humid in summer in Provence in particular and cold winter conditions further north. What would make the journey difficult were factors such as fewer ecclesiastical contacts in the north and therefore less support the further they travelled; injuries arising in the course of travelling; local contexts and leaders; language barriers and local politics and customs.

What would make the journey dangerous would be the activity of brigands; fractious and self-seeking noblemen encountered en route; soldiers and conflict (especially related to Neustria); desperate travellers encountered on the roads; unavoidable forests with potentially dangerous wildlife; and treachery, political rivalry and intrigue at Merovingian courts.

What made the journey as long as it was (nine months or so) were delays in delivering Gregory's letters to various ecclesiastics and patrons, the need to gain Brunhild's support, and Candidus's activities connected with raising revenue from the Frankish papal estates. However, the longest detour – to Tours – seems to have been Augustine's own decision, and it was possibly necessary to obtain the support of Frankish clergy from Tours as translators and preachers of the gospel.

Following Augustine's return from Rome, perhaps in late summer of 596, the missionaries were expected to cultivate fresh contacts in Provence, Burgundy and Austrasia; Gregory appears to have expressed no initial interest in the kingdom of Neustria. The pope's greatly increased range of networks is one significant measure of Augustine's success.

Augustine had no previous experience either of being a bishop (as his letter to Gregory from Canterbury shows) or of diplomatic relations at the highest level of international political power. Gregory the Great, who authored the mission, was clearly skilled in both, yet even he seems initially to have made a significant miscalculation regarding the support for and the status of the mission. In contrast, Augustine effectively secured the co-operation and resources that were needed for the journey to England.

By 601 Gregory would be sending reinforcements to England as the mission spread; not only had his network in Francia enlarged, so had the quality of his information, both in relation to the English, and also concerning the Frankish Church. By the early seventh century papal influence across Francia surpassed that of the Roman Emperor in Constantinople. The Catholic Church in the West was proving increasingly adept at reaching places where the Emperor's legions were no longer able to go.

Notes

1 Gregory the Great, Book XI, Letter 61, To Clotaire, King of the Franks, www.newadvent.org/fathers/360211061.htm.
2 Hugh O'Reilly, *The Legend of the Ermine Lady*, www.traditioninaction.org/religious/h070rp.Ermine.html.
3 Christopher Donaldson, *The Great English Pilgrimage: From Rome to Canterbury*, Norwich: Canterbury Press, 1995, p. 92.
4 David Hill et al., 'Quentovic Defined', *Antiquity* 64 (1990), pp. 51–8.
5 Michel Philippe, 'The Canche Estuary (Pas-de-Calais, France) from the early Bronze Age to the emporium of Quentovic: A traditional trading place between south east England and the Continent', in Peter Clark (ed.), *Bronze Age Connections: Cultural Contact in Prehistoric Europe*, Oxford: Oxbow Books, 2009, pp. 68–79.
6 Bede, *Ecclesiastical History* I.25.

PART 3

Augustine's Mission in England

8

Anglo-Saxon England in 597

The Coming of the Saxons

Roman Christianity had experienced a long and often uneasy relationship with the Imperial State since the middle of the first century. Scarcely a century lay between Constantine's conversion to Christianity in 312 and the final withdrawal of Roman influence and oversight from the British Isles in c. 410. The immediate cause of the abandonment of Britain was the siege of Rome by Alaric, King of the Goths in 408, the first time in more than six centuries that Rome had fallen to a foreign invader.

In reality, however, Britain had been in a state of rebellion against the Emperor since 406. On the last day of December that year several Germanic tribes crossed the frozen Rhine and overran Roman defences, delivering a blow to the Western Empire from which it never recovered. At the time of this invasion, the provinces of Britain were themselves in a revolt that ended with Flavius Claudius Constantinus (known as the English Constantine) declaring himself the Western Emperor early in 407. Fearing a Germanic invasion of Britain, and desperate for some sense of security in a world in crisis, Constantine moved swiftly, crossing the English Channel to establish himself in Gaul, taking with him all of the mobile troops left in Britain. Although he was recognized by Emperor Honorius in 409, a combination of dwindling political support and mounting military setbacks led to Constantine's abdication in 411. He was captured and executed, leaving the British provinces without any first line military protection in the early fifth century.

Christianity was formally recognized as licit within the Roman Empire by the Edict of Milan in 313, but did not achieve the status of sole imperial religion until 400, less than a decade before the Roman abandonment of Britain. As a consequence the Romano-British Church was neither robust nor deeply rooted at the time of the first migrations of Saxons, Jutes and Frisians to England, and the bleak picture of invasions by barbarians, sweeping away all traces of Romano-British civilization like an earthquake, came to define this period as 'the Dark Ages'.[1] Gibbon offered an explanation for the almost total absence of historical records in England between 410 and the arrival of Augustine in 597: 'the Saxon warriors could not write to record their deeds, and the British who could saw little reason to record the ruin of their country'.[2]

A century passed after these first invasions before the Anglo-Saxons came to dominate the centre of the country. 'Who were the people who now inhabited Britain? Gildas states many of the native Britons had fled the eastern lands of former Roman Britannia or had been enslaved. The same word – *wealh* – is used in early Anglo-Saxon law to mean both "Welshman" (i.e. Briton) and "slave".'[3]

If King Arthur existed outside the stories of romantic legend, it would be in this period that his exploits against the Anglo-Saxons took place. (Geoffrey of Monmouth suggested the year of Arthur's death as 542, some 55 years before Augustine's landing in Kent.)

The Romano-British Church did not disappear overnight following the withdrawal of Roman interests from Britain. Long after the Saxon arrivals in the fifth century some British priests and monks continued to serve their local Christian communities. Pagan Kent at the close of the sixth century was a kingdom with place-names commemorating the cults of Woden, Thiw and others. However, there is evidence of the survival of Christianity in rural Kent in local place-names such as Eccles – *ecclesia* – near Rochester. Augustine's discovery of a shrine dedicated to someone called Sixtus (either at Eccles or St Osyth's in Essex) indicates something of the tenacity of Romano-British Christianity in the southeast of England.[4]

Sixtus was apparently a Romano-British Christian, but his later adherents knew nothing of his story – whether he had met a martyr's death, whether there was a liturgy performed in his honour or whether he had performed miracles. He was venerated for generations without any formal church or priestly supervision before Augustine, as the former Roman Church hierarchy (such as it was) had been extinguished in the eastern parts of former Britannia.[5]

Recent genetic studies indicate that the indigenous Romano-British population was more widespread in Anglo-Saxon areas of England such as Kent than previously accepted, and therefore greater continuity may have been the case than earlier authors have suggested.[6] Even so, most people living in the east of England in 597, apart from Queen Bertha and the royal entourage, would have been entirely unaware of the religion of Rome.

Episcopal oversight for the British remnant in Kent over the two centuries following the Roman withdrawal should have come from those closest – the Frankish bishops across the English Channel. Although Arles had maintained a loose oversight over Britain during the Roman administration, the ancient dioceses of Rouen and Rheims were closer – close enough to be visible from the shores of Kent. Pope Gregory cites the failure of the French bishops to extend apostolic oversight as his reason for launching the mission to England from Rome and not Francia.[7]

By the time of Augustine's arrival in 597, aside from Saint Martin's Church that served as Queen Bertha's royal chapel, there was effectively nothing left of the old Romano-Christian dispensation on which to build.

Mission, Mythology and Salvation

The initial spread of Christianity in England was to prove slow; conversion was effected first at the highest level on the basis of social stratification, but the mass of the populace was much less prepared to abandon old practices and beliefs. Coercion, which was the preferred model of the Roman Empire, was to prove an unfeasible option in the social structure of the Anglo-Saxon kingdoms.

Augustine's initial experience of the pagan world and its religious beliefs before setting out from Rome was restricted to ancient Roman and eastern forms, such as the cults of Mithras and Isis; the world-view and practices of the Anglo-Saxons were much less known. The cross and icon of Christ that Augustine's party carried with them were alien to the religious art and mythology of their Anglo-Saxon hosts.

The Anglo-Saxons were very conscious of their roots, whether ancestral or mythological. They still looked towards the Continent and would do so for many generations – heroes like Beowulf were all Danes or Swedes – or even further east for their origins. Both English and German appreciation of such tenacious links, still strong some 300 years after the Anglo-Saxon invasions, serve as a reminder that ideas are almost indestructible, that folk memory is tough and that the human mind in general prefers the security of tradition to the uncertainty of what is new. Even before all England was declared 'Christian', Anglo-Saxon converts were sending missionaries such as Boniface to Germany to convert their near relatives, and the emotional depth of feeling was, 'We are of one blood and one bone.'

Such was the mythological world that awaited Augustine and his mission on the shores of Kent in the spring of 597. However, the Norse gods and those who fashioned their lives by them were already old and tired and spent by the time Augustine set foot in England. From the perspective of history the pagan gods were destroyed not at Ragnarök, but by the coming of a new set of beliefs in the form of Christianity.

Securing a Passage to England

Augustine's missionaries were not the only travellers in 597 to make the journey from Quentovic's trading emporium to the shores of the Wantsum Channel. Archaeological evidence indicates that significant cross-Channel trading connections developed throughout the sixth century between Kent and Francia, across the Channel, and Kent may have gained a monopoly on trade with some elements of the Frankish kingdom. This may suggest the existence of a Frankish fleet to enforce its authority when necessary.[8]

As winter turned to spring, bringing with it warmer weather and longer daylight hours, the trading vessels at Quentovic would be loaded with high-value trade goods in preparation for the first Channel crossing of the year. Surplus ships able to transport a party of up to 40 men and their baggage to the shores of Kent would be hard to find. How would Augustine manage to persuade one or more skippers to take such a large party across the Channel, in boats already crammed with cargo at the start of a new trading season? Here the support of the Frankish rulers, whether Brunhild or Chlothar II, would have been essential, either in commandeering the vessels they needed or paying for the passage on their behalf, particularly as a party of 40 people and their goods would need more than one ship for crossing to England.

The Channel Crossing

Whatever the means of securing a passage during the fifth and sixth centuries, rowing and the tides rather than wind and sail provided the major means of propulsion for the vessels. Even the shortest Channel crossing, beginning at Cap Gris Nez, would have been perilous. Only a few decades later Peter, the first abbot of Saint Peter and Saint Paul (later Saint Augustine's Abbey in Canterbury), was drowned in a bay known as Amfleat (Ambleteuse) while on a mission to Francia.[9]

Cross-Channel navigation made great demands on a skipper's seamanship and required long apprenticeship of the kind that took a family business or a guild several generations to accumulate. A ship's captain needed extensive and accurate knowledge of weather lore and local conditions and an intimate knowledge of a very complex system of tidal currents and changes caused by the lunar cycle. The skipper also needed an excellent memory for water depths, inshore shoals and reefs, landmarks and oral seamanship traditions.

Arriving at Quentovic and negotiating a passage to Kent, Augustine's journey would take the missionaries up the coast to Cap Gris Nez before turning west for England. The endurance required to row from Cap Gris Nez on the French coast to Dover would have been considerable, a journey of ten hours even on a calm sea. An 18-oar planked boat in calm water could expect to achieve a top performance of 6 knots (11 km per hour) for about half an hour at a stretch. An average and more achievable speed would have been about 2.5 knots (4.6 km/hour), insufficient to make adequate headway against tidal currents.[10]

A start-out from shore would need to begin about four hours after high water, heading west away from the cliffs of Cap Gris Nez. Additional time would have been needed for Augustine's journey that began further south at Quentovic. On a clear day, the view of the Dover coastline from the cliffs above the Cap appears deceptively close. However, it would take five hours of rowing, assisted by southwesterly tidal currents, for the Shakespeare Cliffs at Dover to come into view on the starboard bow. Turning north and paddling towards the Kent coast, they would pick up the northeast running currents and make landfall at Dover three hours later, nine hours out from the Frankish coast if conditions were perfect. The ruins of an old Roman lighthouse still remain standing on the chalk cliffs.

Continuing northeast inshore on a rising tide for another four hours, the Goodwin Sands, a ten-mile shoal lying six miles off Deal and a graveyard for maritime vessels, represented a considerable hazard in poor weather. Passing Julius Caesar's 54 BC landing-place at present-day Deal would bring the ship to a line of cliffs that identifies the Isle of Thanet and Pegwell Bay.

After 13 hours out from the Frankish coast, there might not be sufficient daylight to negotiate further into the Wantsum

Channel. The tide would also be running against the ship so that a safe anchorage overnight would have been essential. Should the skipper wish to continue towards Canterbury or through the Wantsum into the Thames Estuary, the journey could be undertaken on a rising tide the following day.

Augustine's Landing and Message to King Aethelberht

Bede records that, upon landing: 'Augustine sent to Aethelberht to say that he had come from Rome bearing the best of news . . . On hearing this the king ordered them to remain on the island where they had landed and be provided with all things necessary until he had decided what to do about them.'[11]

It seems clear that the missionaries did not proceed directly to Canterbury; rather, the ship or ships in which Augustine and his party travelled to Kent made landfall somewhere in the Wantsum estuary. Bede provided an unusually detailed description of the Isle of Thanet and believed that Augustine and his companions had landed there. The archaeological and historical evidence,[12] however, favours Richborough, which was also a small island in the Wantsum near to Thanet and the main destination since Roman times for travellers to Kent. A small haven at Thanet provided temporary anchorage for ships travelling on the following day into the Thames Estuary. Richborough was also part of Aethelberht's estates; Thanet was not. Later associations linking Augustine with Richborough are strong; a century or so after Augustine's arrival in Kent, a chapel was dedicated to the saint within Richborough Fort to commemorate his landing there.

Whatever their exact landing-place, some local means would have been needed to carry a message to Canterbury on the following day. How did Augustine manage to send a message to Aethelberht? And what factors may have influenced Aethelberht's response?

In practical terms, Augustine's message to the king would be conveyed by river – the Roman roads were little used and not maintained; in contrast, travel by boat over some distance was the predominant method of transport, usually faster and safer than travel on foot. A local vessel from the island would have carried one or two of the Frankish interpreters to Canterbury, delivering the message verbally on Augustine's behalf. This would also give Aethelberht the most complete picture of the landing party, its composition and its purpose. By Augustine's second day in Kent, a message would have reached Canterbury that a high-status delegation from Rome, including a bishop, monks and Frankish priests, had landed on the coast and wished to meet with the king.

Reactions to Augustine's Message

It seems clear from Bede's account that even though Bertha had earnestly requested and prayed for support to convert Kent's pagan Anglo-Saxons, the actual arrival of the party of missionaries was unexpected; on the contrary, the royal court seems to have been thrown into disarray at the news. Bertha, having waited and prayed for more than two decades for the arrival of a mission, was clearly unaware that such a party was on its way to Kent. Later events in Canterbury confirm that the queen welcomed the arrival of Augustine and the missionaries and no doubt particularly the Frankish priests. The hospitality that was shown to the missionaries at Saint Martin's Church soon led to its extension. Nothing suggests that Augustine's arrival was not welcomed.

Other factors may equally account for the unusual response of the Kentish royal household, particularly the high status of the unexpected missionaries. Visitors of rank, and from Merovingian Francia in particular, would not be strangers to Kent. Aethelberht, following the practice of the Merovingians, had married outside his own people, turning away from the daughters of his own Anglo-Saxon aristocracy to take a bride from the Frankish royal court. Francia apparently held some undefined form of hegemony over the Kentish kingdom, and this may have opened the way for the match. Bertha would also have kept contact with her mother in Tours (or Le Mans), sending and receiving messages through court officials. Trade relations involving merchants, messengers and diplomats would have been part of a steady stream of contact between the royal court and the Continent. Aethelberht's royal court was far from unsophisticated, as contemporary artefacts, particularly jewellery, clearly show.

However, a large party of monks and lay brothers from Rome, led by a bishop on a mission commissioned by the pope, arriving together with priests and lay clerks sent by a Merovingian royal court, would have been a party quite unprecedented in both scale and status in Kent at this time. Hasty arrangements would need to be made for suitable accommodation and hospitality at the royal palace in Canterbury and additional supplies brought in from the king's various estates. Aethelberht's leading men and counsellors also needed to be consulted. Confusion in Canterbury on receiving Augustine's message would be understandable. Bede records: 'Augustine sent to Aethelberht to say that he had come from Rome bearing the best of news, namely the sure and certain promise of eternal joys in heaven and an endless kingdom with the living and true God to those who received it.'[13]

The practice of the Christian faith was not unknown in Canterbury. Queen Bertha had arrived in Kent as a Christian, together with her chaplain Liudhard and her personal entourage. Over the next two decades or more, she had drawn together a small Christian community and built a small chapel dedicated to Saint Martin. Gregory knew nothing of this in 596 when he sent Augustine. The pope may have assumed that the situation facing them would be on the model of other missions closer to Rome. In Gregory's view this approach consisted of preaching to pagans and ill-instructed Christians of less than acceptable manners.[14]

In addition to making temporary arrangements for Augustine and his party's immediate needs, the next few days would allow the king time to call together his leading men and decide how they should respond to Augustine. However, while Aethelberht may have been reluctant to allow the party to continue directly to Canterbury, he clearly believed that the place where they had landed could provide everything that Augustine's party needed for shelter and sustenance.

Richborough was the nearest port to Francia, and this small island, containing a fort, buildings and adequate supplies, was Augustine's most likely landing-place. A possible explanation for the initial sequence of events is that Augustine landed – and remained – at Richborough until summoned by King Aethelberht. It appears that the island of Richborough, with little if any break in habitation since the withdrawal of Roman protection after 410, was able to sustain a local community that engaged in agriculture and fishing and maintained a port and trading station or *wic*.

For Augustine's party the island, and perhaps the fort itself, offered some measure of hospitality as well as shelter while they waited for a meeting with King Aethelberht.[15]

Augustine's Meeting with Aethelberht

Bede records the first face-to-face meeting between the monk–bishop missionary from Rome and the most powerful Anglo-Saxon ruler in England:

> Some days afterwards the king came to the island and, sitting in the open air, commanded Augustine and his comrades thither to talk with him . . . At the king's command they sat down and preached the word of life to himself and his counts [*gesiths*] there present.[16]

Aethelberht apparently needed several days to decide how to respond to Augustine. It would take at least a day or two to gather his leading men to consult and deliberate. The arrival of a large party of people seeking to undertake missionary work had multiple implications, including their ongoing need for support in Canterbury and the impact they might have on the polity, religion and the Anglo-Saxon way of life. Aethelberht needed time to weigh up these considerations with his Christian queen, his inner council of advisers and Bishop Liudhard if he was still living, before meeting with Augustine.

Bede does not record how long Aethelberht deliberated with his council, nor the details of any meetings. However, he does recall that when the king came to the island, he summoned Augustine to meet him 'in the open air' – perhaps to avoid the danger of being overwhelmed by magic, more easily performed indoors.[17]

What might account for Aethelberht's suspicions is that in Anglo-Saxon beliefs and artistic expression visual tricks were a common feature of jewellery design. The square-headed brooches made in Kent during the fifth and sixth centuries show that what appears to be an animal from one point of view suddenly appears as a human face if turned 90 degrees. Something deeper is communicated by this recurring theme in Anglo-Saxon art. Just as a serious play on words might lie beneath a riddle, so brooches can be a play on images: the eye and the ear can both be deceived. For Bede, this encounter stressed the spiritual power of the missionaries and underlined the extent to which the king was simply sunk in pagan superstition. However, it may have been customary for meetings to be held in the open air even among communities living much further afield. Some six years later Augustine, under similar circumstances, met with representatives of the British Church outdoors.

Augustine and Aethelberht met together as representatives of two very different worlds, faiths and ways of life. The missionaries according to Bede came to meet the king chanting Latin Psalms, bearing a silver cross and an icon of Christ painted on a panel in the tradition of narrative, visual imagery. This was integral to Christian worship of the period, but alien to the Anglo-Saxons whose native art was essentially decorative and aniconic.[18]

Icons had their origin in the Roman Empire with Julius Caesar, who mounted two expeditions to the Kentish coast nearly six centuries before Augustine. In the early Christian Church icons were central to the liturgy. Belief in the power of icons grew steadily, so that by the beginning of the fifth century they were carried into battle to protect armies and hung over the gates of cities to ward off adversaries. As Gregory had spent nine years as papal legate to Constantinople and experienced icons in the Eastern Church, their adoption in worship at Saint Andrew's Monastery in Rome seems certain. The icon of Christ carried by the missionaries was therefore deeply significant. When Augustine met Aethelberht bearing a cross and an icon of Christ, he also carried with him the full expectation of Christ's protection.

Augustine's Words to the Anglo-Saxon King

Augustine and his Roman companions had acquired interpreters from the Frankish race according to the command of Pope Gregory. It seems that the Franks, as they shared a common Germanic ancestry with the inhabitants of England, spoke a dialect of Anglo-Saxon. Gregory had the foresight to realize (or perhaps Augustine had pointed this out to the pope on his return to Rome) that no preaching would be possible unless the hearers could understand. Gregory's response to the need for a latter-day 'Pentecost of the Gentiles' was to ask for Frankish priests who could speak both Latin and a Germanic dialect similar to Old English.

Much of the initial conversation may have revolved around traditional comments concerning the journey, a mention that Augustine had made a pilgrimage to the shrine of Saint Martin at Tours, the full support he had received from Bertha's relative, Queen Brunhild, and also others en route; and not least, how the Franks had prospered greatly under Catholic Christianity. The meeting probably lasted a few hours and would have included traditional hospitality of food and drink until the rising tide carried them all upstream to Canterbury.

Bede wrote what he considered the essence of Augustine's message:

Augustine sent to Aethelberht to say that he had come from Rome bearing the best of news, namely the sure and certain promise of eternal joys in heaven and an endless kingdom with the living and true God to those who received it.[19]

It is notable that Bede presents Augustine's missionary preaching as overwhelmingly positive. Despite Pope Gregory's initial model of mission to pagans, what Bede describes is not a direct condemnation of pagan traditions; Aethelberht and his entourage would themselves know well enough where their weaknesses lay. Rather, the certainty of spiritual reward for anyone who received these promises from the Almighty is affirmed – to anyone who reads or hears Bede's account. An endless Kingdom is offered, with resonances of the royal mead-hall, while eternal fellowship with God pointed to the fellowship that would be enjoyed by the king's subjects within the greater Kingdom of the King of kings.

Everyone present heard the translation of Augustine's words from Latin into the Anglo-Saxon tongue so that the king's response, regardless of what he might personally have believed, would have been cautious and measured:

> The words and the promises you bring are fair enough, but because they are new to us and doubtful, I cannot consent to accept them and forsake those beliefs which I and the whole English race have held so long. But as you have come on a long pilgrimage and are anxious, I perceive, to share with us things which you believe to be true and good, we do not wish to do you harm; on the contrary, we will receive you hospitably and provide what is necessary for your support; nor do we forbid you to win all you can to your faith and religion by your preaching.[20]

There can only have been a huge sense of relief on the part of the missionaries on hearing these words. After being bedevilled by their fears of the barbarity of the Anglo-Saxons at the beginning of their journey and then nine months of travel through the heat, rain and cold of the seasons, difficult times and hostile circumstances, what the monks had feared most was, for now, laid to rest with the king's words: We wish you no harm – on the contrary, we welcome you.

Bertha had prayed for this moment for several decades. Aethelberht could scarcely have made a more appropriate response: reassuring, welcoming, generous, statesmanlike but cautious for the sake of his noblemen and for the ancient Saxon beliefs that they shared. Aethelberht had seen the missionaries at first hand, heard Augustine's words, noted his demeanour and had made up his mind. The missionaries would be welcome in Canterbury. At last a beachhead for the mission to Anglo-Saxon Kent had been achieved.

The Wantsum Channel and River Stour to Canterbury

Accompanying the surge of high tide carrying Augustine's party upstream might have been an equally strong upsurge of thanksgiving for their journey to Kent. Augustine especially, with two hours or so to reach Canterbury, might have reflected on the rebellion by some of his companions in Aix and his unexpected return to Rome. Whatever the pope's reaction on seeing his missioner back in Rome again after only a matter of weeks, Augustine had nevertheless returned to Francia with the letters he needed to complete his commission. He had re-engaged his companions and continued the journey, secured support from bishops and monasteries on the way and most significant of all received almost unlimited support from the dowager Queen of Austrasia and Burgundy. Augustine had obtained the assistance of Frankish priests from Tours and secured a safe passage through Neustria to Quentovic. Crossing the English Channel, he had finally brought all his companions safely ashore on the Kent coast. He had not lost one.

Most important of all, Augustine had now received the support of Aethelberht, who had given his permission for the missionaries to continue to Canterbury. Yet, despite the nine months of hard travel that lay behind, his work in Canterbury had only just begun. The biggest challenge now was the conversion and baptism of the king himself, and on this single event hung the success or failure of the mission as conceived by Gregory.

Landing at Fordwich

Three symbols traditionally characterized Anglo-Saxon settlers: the axe for cutting-back the forests, the heavy plough to work the clotted soil, but most significantly their shallow-draught ships. The rivers and the seas played a greater role in Anglo-Saxon life than the roads that had once been strategic during the Roman period. Ports multiplied beyond Canterbury from around 600 onwards – Fordwich, Sarre, Minster, Reculver, Richborough, Sandwich as well as the northeastern *suburbium* of Canterbury itself, where a trading port has been identified on the River Stour.[21]

River and tide permitting, it was at times possible to proceed beyond Fordwich to within a few hundred yards of Canterbury's city wall and continue to Aethelberht's royal complex. The Vikings apparently used this route up the River Stour to sack Canterbury in 1012. It is more likely that the party rowed only as far as Fordwich and from there continued on foot along an ancient Saxon path that is now part of the Stour Valley Walk for the next 1.9 miles (3 km) to Saint Martin's.

The area between Fordwich and Canterbury contained a thriving *wic* or emporium before the seventh century, evidence of Kent's growing trade links with the Continent.[22] The advantage of the Saxon footpath was that the missionaries could walk dry-shod from Fordwich to Canterbury at any time of the year.

On the last stretch of the Saxon path they would come at last into clear view of Canterbury's walls little more than half a mile away. Bede records that Augustine and his companions chanted a litany when they first saw the city: 'We beseech Thee, O Lord, in Thy great mercy, that Thy wrath and anger may be turned away from this city and from Thy holy house, for we have sinned. Alleluia.'[23] What was the reason for this?

Augustine and his Roman companions had been away from their Saint Andrew's community for many months. Most monastic Rules laid down procedures for how monks undertaking a journey should conduct themselves, as the temptations they might face on a journey were numerous. Chapter 67 of Saint Benedict's Rule requires that the community should pray daily for those away on monastery business at the closing prayer of the Divine Office. Correspondingly, those on the journey should also strive to maintain the same daily offices as their home monastery, but this would have been extraordinarily difficult to maintain during Augustine's extended period in Francia. On their return, the monks prostrated themselves in the chapel during the time of prayer, seeking mercy for what they had seen, heard, thought and done while away. For Augustine and his companions, the antiphon for Terce would capture this perfectly: beseeching the Almighty for mercy and not visiting their sin upon the city to which they had come as bearers of the gospel of salvation.

In showing the missionaries singing a penitential prayer in the queen's chapel as an act that would normally mark a return to one's home community at journey's end, Bede may have been making a further point. There was no serious prospect of their return to Rome, and the same could have been true for most of the Frankish priests who accompanied them. Their new monastic community now comprised those companions that Augustine had brought with him and those they would draw to faith in the preaching of Good News. Augustine symbolically declares with these words that Canterbury was now their dwelling-place; Rome was no longer their home.

This is important to Bede as a beneficiary of Augustine's mission that had begun to shape a distinctive 'English nation'. While Gregory receives Bede's lasting gratitude for being the author of the mission to the Anglo-Saxon peoples, it is Augustine who roots the gospel in English soil. What makes Augustine more than Pope Gregory's emissary is that he was the one who not only came but committed himself unreservedly to the English people as a missionary who became, for Bede, 'one of our own'.

Arrival in Canterbury (*Cantwaraburh*)

From earliest times Canterbury has occupied a key role as a centre for trade and communications, as well as for different cultures and religious beliefs. An Iron Age fort at Bigbury near Canterbury once dominated its western approaches. The city's location at the crossways of river and road helped Canterbury achieve pre-eminence in Kent. Upstream and downstream on the Stour, the hills turned this area into a shallow basin. A river ford crossed this hollow plain and until the silting of the Wantsum Channel in the sixteenth century the tidal water of the Wantsum ended at Canterbury. Through this area passed ancient highroads long before the Romans built converging road systems from Lympne, Dover, Reculver and Whitstable.

Roman Canterbury, *Durovernum Cantiacorum*, offered the Romans and those who came before them a strategic location – a place shaped by 'ways' from the west – Salisbury Plain, the Surrey Hills and the North Downs. Cornish tin was carried to Gaul and Belgia via Canterbury. Ancient times saw the Druids walking the 'way' from the west, and pagans then Saxons and Vikings worshipped their gods at this place.[24]

Saxon Cantwaraburh

The Old English *burh* refers to a fortified enclosure of any size, whether a plot of land, a fortress or an enclosure around a royal palace. Canterbury was clearly such a place.[25] In contrast to urbanized Roman Britain, few early Anglo-Saxons seem to have settled within walled towns.

Most Romano-British cities and towns ceased to be important in Britain after 410 and in some instances much earlier.

Archaeological evidence indicates an exodus of the upper classes from Romano-British cities during this period. A few Romano-British towns including Canterbury continued to function until the mid-fifth century, but with the possible exception of Wroxeter none have shown clear evidence of later occupation. The last remaining cities – Bath, Cirencester and Gloucester – were razed by 577–8.

First impressions were not encouraging. Although the missionaries had sufficiently impressed Aethelberht, Canterbury could hardly have inspired the missionaries. As Augustine surveyed Canterbury for the first time from the Saxon path on St Martin's Hill, the city would have presented a scene of almost total devastation. The walls, only completed in 290, were now punctuated by seven derelict gateways and formed little more than a shell enclosing acres of ruins. The layout of the city was already becoming irretrievably lost beneath buildings that had collapsed into the streets, and everywhere vermin-ridden rubble remained uncleared.

There would be scarcely any overlap at all between the patterns of the earlier Roman roads and later medieval streets, and none of the sixth- and seventh-century Saxon *havels* (round houses) excavated in Canterbury stood in any clear relation to the original Roman street layout. They used the well-drained and paved Roman roads merely as a firm floor for a few wood and thatch dwellings.[26]

Despite the urban decay that Augustine had known in his own greatly depopulated Rome, the contrast with late sixth-century Canterbury can hardly be exaggerated. Only the theatre remained standing, now possibly used as a market place, its original purpose unknown to those who lived in or passed through the ruins of the city. The 30 or so wattle and mud *havels* that existed were small and makeshift in comparison to the earlier Roman structures. Only Aethelberht's royal hall, which served as the gathering-place of Aethelberht's tribal warriors, would have given the impression of the seat of the most powerful king in England; and it is by no means certain that this was within the walls of Canterbury itself.

Location of Aethelberht's Royal Palace

On Augustine's arrival, the obvious place to lodge foreign dignitaries would have been within or near to the royal complex. But where was it? Archaeologists have yet to locate an early royal hall in Canterbury that would seem capable of offering hospitality commensurate with their numbers and status, but two potential locations have been proposed.

Historian Nicholas Brooks has suggested that the decaying Roman theatre may have been used as the early royal centre of Cantwaraburh, providing a fitting seat for Aethelberht. Here the kings of Kent, the *Oisingas*, met with their Jutish folk and settled matters of justice, warfare and politics. It is therefore conceivable that there was a royal residence with permanent buildings and even some permanent staff in the city.[27]

Brooks points out that at Canterbury after the Roman buildings had collapsed, the Roman theatre was the largest and most visible structure still standing in the city. Here people would have gathered as they entered the city from the south and east. Here too the kings of Kent may have met with their people, the *Cantware*. The three-dozen sunken buildings clustered to the rear of the ruined Roman theatre were multi-purpose structures, perhaps used to house a variety of craft activities and workers.[28] As the city itself was part of Aethelberht's royal estate, it is possible that the few *havels* excavated within the city walls were associated with the supervision and protection of the king's grain-stores.

A second possible location for Aethelberht's royal hall complex lies to the east of the old city walls, near to the site of Saint Martin's Church. The earliest royal regional centres in Kent were not based on former Roman walled centres. Old English names ending in 'ge' describe a centre for a district or region, as in Lyminge or Sturry (*Sturigao*). Sturry was superseded in the 590s by a new royal hall, located nearer to Canterbury, when Aethelberht acceded to the throne.

During this period both St Martin's Hill and Sturry (a small town 4 km north of Canterbury on the former Roman road that led to the fort at Reculver) may have been involved in an emerging trading and manufacturing complex outside the walls of Canterbury. A trading centre – *wic* – may have stretched from below St Martin's Hill to the port of Fordwich, located between the Stour River and the Saxon Way path from Fordwich to St Martin's Hill.[29]

Archaeologists Margaret Sparks and Tim Tatton-Brown have suggested that the commanding position offered by Saint Martin's Hill would have made this a credible location for a timber palace complex and royal hall near to Saint Martin's Chapel. Also, Saint Martin's remained a royal manor until the ninth century.[30] This area is also set away from the low-lying city and the River Stour that passes through it, while providing a commanding view over the town and also the approach to Canterbury from the northeast. Although no archaeological evidence for a royal hall has so far been found, early Anglo-Saxon buildings did exist between Saint Martin's Church and the Roman Watling Street that linked Canterbury to Richborough.[31] This would have been a good location for lodging Augustine's missionaries until the cathedral and abbey were built.

Bede records that the king showed extremely generous hospitality to Augustine: 'He gave them a dwelling in the city of Canterbury, which was the chief city of all his dominions, and in accordance with his promise, he granted them provisions and did not refuse them freedom to preach.'[32] Bede could be referring to their initial accommodation near to Saint Martin's, part of the king's royal complex, which could have provided accommodation for the missionaries until the king granted permission for a cathedral to be built within the walls of the city.

Augustine and his companions had reached their goal, and they had been welcomed by the king. How would they now proceed with the mission of bringing Good News to the *Angli* of Kent?

Notes

1 Richard Church (ed.), *A Portrait of Canterbury*, London: Hutchinson, 1953, p. 28.

2 Edward Gibbon, *The Decline and Fall of the Roman Empire*, London: Everyman's Library, Vol. IV, 1994, p. 59.

3 Caroline Alexander, *Lost Gold of the Dark Ages: War, Treasure, and the Mystery of the Saxons*, New York: National Geographic Society, 2011, p. 49.

4 Richard Gameson (ed.), *St Augustine and the Conversion of England*, Stroud: Sutton Publishing Ltd, 1999, p. 146.

5 Robin Fleming, *Britain after Rome: The Fall and Rise 400–1070*, London: Allen Lane (Penguin), 2010, p. 132.

6 C. Capelli et al., 'A Y Chromosome Census of the British Isles', *Current Biology* 13 (2003), p. 979.

7 Gregory the Great, Book IV, Letter 59.

8 Stuart Brookes and Sue Harrington, *The Kingdom and People of Kent, AD 400–1066*, Stroud: History Press, 2010, p. 47.

9 Bede, *Ecclesiastical History* I.33.

10 David Perkins, 'Prehistoric Maritime Traffic in the Dover Strait and Wantsum: Some thoughts as to the vessels and their crews', *Archaeologia Cantiana* 26 (2006), p. 286.

11 Bede, *Ecclesiastical History* I.25.

12 Tony Wilmott, 'Richborough, More than a Roman Fort', *Current Archaeology* 257, August 2011, p. 23.

13 Bede, *Ecclesiastical History* I.25.

14 R. A. Markus, *Gregory the Great and His World*, Cambridge: Cambridge University Press, 1997, p. 47.

15 Gameson, *St Augustine*, p. 11.

16 Bede, *Ecclesiastical History* I.25.

17 Richard Rudgley, *Barbarians: Secrets of the Dark Ages*, Oxford: Channel 4 Books, 2002, p. 158.

18 Gameson, *St Augustine*, p. 18.

19 Bede, *Ecclesiastical History* I.25.

20 Bede, *Ecclesiastical History* I.25.

21 Timothy Tatton-Brown, *Canterbury History Guide*, Stroud: Sutton Publishing Ltd, 1994, p. 13.

22 Jonathan Rady, 'Excavations at St Martin's Hill, Canterbury, 1984–85', *Archaeologia Cantiana* 104 (1987), pp. 123–218.

23 Bede, *Ecclesiastical History* I.25.

24 Michael A. Green, *St Augustine of Canterbury*, London: Janus Publishing, 1997, pp. 5–6.

25 Jeremy Haslam, *Early Medieval Towns in Britain*, Princes Risborough: Shire Publications Ltd, 2010, p. 19.

26 Nicholas Brooks, *The Early History of the Church of Canterbury: Christ Church from 597 to 1066*, London and New York: Leicester University Press, 1984, pp. 21–2.

27 Brooks, *Early History*, p. 25.

28 Fleming, *Britain after Rome*, p. 185.

29 John H. Williams (ed.), *The Archaeology of Kent to AD 800*, Kent History Project 8, Woodbridge: The Boydell Press and Kent County Council, 2007, p. 244.

30 Williams, *Archaeology of Kent*, p. 237.

31 Margaret Sparks and Timothy Tatton-Brown, 'The History of the Vill of St Martin's, Canterbury', *Archaeologia Cantiana* 104 (1987), pp. 171–8.

32 Bede, *Ecclesiastical History* I.25.

9

Augustine's Mission to Kent

Bede offers neither a timeline nor a clear sequence of how Augustine's mission unfolded during 597–604. His source, Albinus, died in 732, a year after Bede completed his *Ecclesiastical History*. Bede's account of events in Canterbury shows that almost nothing of the mission had been committed to writing and very little beyond a broad outline survived in oral tradition at the abbey and cathedral priory. The absence of a scriptorium in the missionaries' early years in Canterbury may partly account for this. Nevertheless, four broad stages of development of the mission may be discerned during Augustine's lifetime.

The first stage begins with Augustine's arrival in Canterbury and concludes with the baptism of King Aethelberht (by tradition Pentecost June 597) and a large number of his kinsmen during the midwinter festival on 25 December 597.

The second stage sees Laurentius and Peter returning to Rome in 598 to petition Pope Gregory for reinforcements. Peter and Laurentius returned to Kent, and Augustine began preparations for building a cathedral in Canterbury.

The third stage is marked by the arrival of high-powered reinforcements from Rome in the persons of Justus, Abbot Mellitus (possibly the leader of the group), Paulinus and Rufianus. They brought with them a pallium from Gregory, who formally recognized Augustine as archbishop (Frankish 'metropolitan'). They also brought letters from Gregory to Aethelberht, Bertha and Augustine, relics from the shrine of Saint Sixtus for British Christians in Kent (at Augustine's request), books and manuscripts for a school, church plate and furnishings for worship.

During this period, Augustine also prepared the way for the abbey by consecrating and preparing a piece of ground granted for this purpose by the king. The cathedral was completed and consecrated for worship. Augustine and Laurentius, together with most of the Frankish interpreters, occupied the priory. Abbot Peter and most of the Italian contingent remained at Saint Martin's to oversee work on the abbey.

In the last stage, Augustine and Aethelberht began to look outwards to other Saxon kingdoms and British territories, reaching out to the British Church. After unsuccessful encounters with the British bishops, Augustine returned to Canterbury to consecrate Laurentius, Justus and Mellitus as bishops. He died soon afterwards in 604.

Queen Bertha

Bertha was the most significant person in Kent for Augustine's mission to the *Angli* and her support was crucial at almost every stage. She was the eldest daughter of Charibert I, Merovingian king of Paris until 567. A condition of her marriage to Aethelberht was that Bertha would continue to practise her Christian faith, and she brought Bishop Liudhard as her chaplain. Bertha built a chapel, which she dedicated to Saint Martin of Tours, and apparently gathered there a small congregation. She prayed in this chapel for a mission to arrive and convert the *Angli*.

Nearly three decades passed before Augustine landed on the small island of Richborough. The timing could not have been more fortuitous. Bertha's chaplain had died by 597, and support from the profoundly compromised Neustrian church was not forthcoming. Augustine had also taken a significant detour to Tours and knew the significance of Saint Martin and something of Bertha's life in Francia before her marriage. By the second year of the mission (598) Gregory was already aware of Bertha's generous support for Augustine. The pope wrote not only that her good deeds were recognized in Rome where she was earnestly prayed for, but also that news of her generosity had even reached Constantinople and the ears of the Byzantine Emperor.[1]

Bertha's desire for a mission to the *Angli* was undoubtedly sincere. She was more concerned for the welfare of the people of Aethelberht's kingdom than for merely extending the relics-based cult of Saint Martin to Kent. There is no indication that any of Saint Martin's relics were ever brought to Canterbury – either by Bertha at the time of her marriage or by Augustine on his departure from Tours. Her yearning was more for the healing of bodies and souls than for the veneration of ancient bones. This made it possible for Augustine to focus the mission on the poor and needy.

Bertha was also acutely aware of the appalling consequences that a warrior culture brought upon the whole of Anglo-Saxon society. She also knew that there was an alternative: her younger sisters were nuns in Tours and Poitiers, and monastic life opened up another way of life for high and low born alike. Monasteries also provided education for boys, making possible an alternative to a warrior's life and death for those who had neither the skills nor the stomach for such a trade. In Kent much needed to be done among the *Angli*, and through Augustine much could be achieved.

Augustine's Conception of the Mission

Augustine was aware that there were tensions between alternative approaches to mission and church organization. One was the familiar Roman and Continental model, organized on a territorial basis having a bishop overseeing a diocese and exercising the authority of office, supported by secular priests. The other was an Irish and British model, essentially monastic, fundamentally rural, and more suited to going out among the peasant farmers than a bishop and clergy of a city-based cathedral. Augustine's own mission in Canterbury was a careful reworking of both of these. He drew on the examples of both Martin of Tours and Pope Gregory, who believed that the qualities of a bishop merged with those of a monk, and that an active pastoral ministry could be integrated into a life of contemplation.

Augustine continued the Roman and Continental practice of a cathedral in a see city, while at the same time going out to the rural population as Martin had done in the countryside around Tours. He recognized that having a monastery integrated into the life of a cathedral would make more sense for a kinship-based rural English society than a Continental model of bishop-and-diocese, mainly organized to serve an urban centre. This proved to be the case, and by the seventh century a bishop-abbot in England would be regarded as the father of his family, like any Saxon lord, so that the cultural resonances for the emerging Church in England were strong.

In contrast, the rural forms of Irish and British monasticism were ultimately less able to adapt to the changing needs of city-based polities already emerging across seventh-century England. Within four decades of arriving on Lindisfarne, the Irish monks withdrew to Iona following the outcome of the Synod of Whitby (664). Ultimately this may have been less about losing the debate over Easter and more about the inability of Irish monasticism to adapt to a new and rapidly changing political, social and increasingly urban landscape.

The Missionaries' Common Life

Together the monks and priests, lay brothers and lay clerks comprised the largest group of Christians worshipping at Saint Martin's, overwhelming the small chapel, so that an extension of the nave was imperative. It was also essential that the lay brothers were kept fully occupied on meaningful work that contributed to the overall mission. They would not be expected to preach and teach, but they possessed the building skills essential to undertake an extension of the chapel, particularly skills for making bricks and roof tiles and working with stone. These were not skills found among Aethelberht's subjects at this time. What rapidly took shape was the largest brick, tile and stone edifice of any kind to be built in Canterbury and probably in the whole of England since the fifth century.

The missionaries' life together was a convincing witness to the people of Kent, their manner of life distinctive from the start and integral to the way in which they conducted the Kentish mission. Bede records:

> As soon as they entered the dwelling place allotted to them, they began to imitate the way of life of the apostles and of the primitive church. They were constantly engaged in prayers, in vigils and fasts; they preached the word of life to as many as they could; they despised all worldly things as foreign to them; they accepted only the necessaries of life from those whom they taught; in all things they practised what they preached and kept themselves prepared to endure adversities, even to the point of dying for the truths they proclaimed.[2]

However, before the Church was granted official status by the king, what Bede described as 'apostolic simplicity' on the part of the missionaries was hardly optional as they had few resources at their disposal. Bede also mentions that what drew converts to faith was the missionaries' poverty and prayer, drawn together as they were for mutual support in a foreign land. At first the missionaries lived their lives very much in the public gaze, having no separate monastic garth and cloister, refectory, chapter house or any of the usual monastic buildings. By living simply, unified in a shared life of poverty and prayer, eating frugally (in contrast to the lavish fare offered in the nearby royal hall) the monks made a strong impression, even though this initially produced few imitators.[3]

The king had received the missionaries as a high-ranking foreign legation, but their dependence on the king's generosity could soon create problems with his inner circle as the missionaries began to extend their stay from months to years. In the very early stages their meals would be taken in the king's hall along with the queen, Aethelberht's advisers, warriors, traders and the never-ending stream of visitors and supplicants for the king's generosity and support.

The monks ate one meal a day. The difference between the carousing and all-night mead quaffing by the king's warriors and the sober, disciplined life of the missionaries could not have passed unnoticed. For Augustine, to eat at table with the king and queen would make a significant impact on his standing among status-conscious English nobility. The Anglo-Saxon aristocracy lived in constant competition for lands, property and status symbols, such as gold rings, weaponry and expensive ornamentation, which were dispensed lavishly by the king to reward loyalty or bravery. By renouncing personal possessions and holding all things in common, the contrast between the values and lifestyle of the monks and the king's warriors was stark.

Aethelberht's Baptism

Once settled near Saint Martin's Chapel, Augustine turned his attention to the most urgent challenge: the conversion of the king. Until Aethelberht himself was baptized, few if any of his nobles and warriors would receive baptism and the mission would make no progress. The strength of solidarity between Aethelberht and his noblemen, the prestige of dining at the royal table, the dependence on favours and reward from the king and the common adherence to ancestral beliefs would all conspire against conversion to a new religion if the king himself did not first receive baptism.

However, there were several factors prompting Aethelberht to turn to Christianity. On the broader stage the Kentish dynasty, now in its fourth generation, had already passed its zenith. Making a Continental alliance with Frankish Christian kingdoms, cemented through his royal union with Bertha, was an increasingly attractive proposition for Aethelberht. Politically, becoming a Christian was not simply a matter of personal belief for

Anglo-Saxon kings; conversion had serious political ramifications, as Aethelberht's initial response to Augustine suggests:

> The words and the promises you bring are fair enough, but because they are new to us and doubtful, I cannot consent to accept them and forsake those beliefs which I and the whole English race have held so long.[4]

A change of religion involved transformations in culture with major implications for a ruler's relationship with his followers and family, the living as well as the departed. Conversion to Christianity for a Saxon king directly affected culture, tradition, family and power politics, not only his personal faith. A king was more than a warrior-ruler with a central role in society; he also held sacral, possibly totemic, status. Saxon kings traced their ancestry to pagan gods, notably Woden, and held a shamanic role as mediator between their people and their gods on whose support the prosperity of the kingdom was believed to depend. Shrines and temples across the country reinforced the power of the old religion.

As a semi-religious figure, political leader and warlord, a king had great authority to introduce new religious customs. Conversely, he needed very good reasons for introducing radical changes and abandoning traditional beliefs, since the responsibility for the welfare of his people – material and spiritual, as dispensed by the old gods – rested squarely on his shoulders. The king had to move in harmony with his nobles in order to address the broader political implications of change or risk losing his kingdom.[5]

There were also considerable positive benefits to weigh in favour of turning to Christianity. Although Aethelberht's conversion meant a dramatic break with the past and its traditions and possibly the loss of some pagan allies, it clearly offered the king the opportunity to become part of the late Roman Christian empire, thus joining an even more powerful network – one that was beginning to engulf the older, independent political institutions.

Christianity arrived in England in a period of intense and brutal political competition. Throughout the country, the prospects for material benefits and social advancement were significant motivators for Anglo-Saxon leaders. Some kings undoubtedly viewed conversion to Christianity as another step towards power and wealth, as the new religion brought with it impressive writing skills for law making and building technologies for making large-scale statements of power and prestige. Missionaries from the post-Roman Christian world were able to capitalize on this and help newly converted kings administer their kingdoms more efficiently for greater financial advantage. This would not have escaped Augustine either.

For Aethelberht, the option of receiving Christianity from distant Rome carried fewer political implications than receiving spiritual oversight from neighbouring France, particularly as the Frankish bishops were heavily dependent on the patronage of their rulers (as indeed Augustine was upon Aethelberht).

The outcome of the king's conversion in economic terms opened better access to and interaction with a wider Continental world, creating wealth through both trade and taxation. Although by 430 Roman coinage had ceased to circulate in post-Roman Britain, by 630 gold coins were being minted in Kent, and the promise of growing trade links and greater prosperity for the kingdom was not disappointed.[6]

Implications of the King's Baptism for Augustine

If conversion was advantageous for Aethelberht, for Augustine the king's conversion was paramount; the survival of the mission depended upon it. A Christian king would give the new bishop and his entourage privileged official status, now able to operate under the protection of a powerful patron. This reflected the pattern of the growth of Christianity in Rome under Constantine I. Latin Christendom also provided the necessary cultural shell in which commerce and statehood could develop. The importance of the Augustinian mission lay, not in forging a cultural chain and so binding Kent with Francia and beyond into a large Christian civilization, but in bringing membership for England within a pan-European network of culture, trade and ideas.[7]

When the moment finally came Bede records that, 'At the last, the king, as well as others, believed and was baptized . . .' Strangely, Gregory's letters directly mention only Aethelberht's baptism. We know nothing of 'the others', but Bede was possibly referring to the warriors of Aethelberht's personal guard and his chief officers, who would have been chosen for their complete loyalty to the king. Although Bede does not record where or when the baptisms took place, he does suggest that it was soon after Augustine's arrival. An auspicious date would be essential for so significant a baptism. Thomas Elmham, a late-medieval writer and monk at Saint Augustine's Abbey, believed that the king was baptized on Whit Sunday, 2 June 597 in Saint Martin's Church.[8] The king squatted in a tank-sized baptismal font while Augustine administered the traditional rite, pouring water from a scallop shell three times over the king's head in the Name of the Trinity.

The six-month period between the king's baptism and the conversion of substantial numbers of the king's closest followers would have been an anxious time for the royal household, as Aethelberht's chief men debated whether or not to follow their king. Bede records that the king did not coerce his nobles, warriors or subjects to follow his example, and his son and heir Eadbald did not follow Aethelberht's example until after the king's death. However, Bede makes it clear that Aethelberht showed more affection to those who did follow him in baptism, acknowledging them as fellow citizens in the Kingdom of Heaven.[9] For Augustine, the king's baptism now signalled an open door for unhindered witness to the Christian faith.

The turning point for both king and bishop came when a very substantial number of Anglo-Saxons followed Aethelberht and were baptized on 25 December 597. This, too, followed a practice that Augustine had learned from the life of Saint Martin while in Tours. Gregory's own correspondence with the

Patriarch of Alexandria numbers these at 10,000, but this figure may be exaggerated. Bede attributes this outcome to the pure life and gracious promises of Augustine and his companions, which were verified by many miracles, drawing many to hear the Word, forsake their heathen ways and enter into fellowship with Christ's Holy Church.[10]

The way was now open for extending the mission to the whole of Aethelberht's kingdom. Within four years – by 601, if not sooner – Augustine needed to call for reinforcements from Rome. What is notable is that he did not seek reinforcements from the most obvious source – the Frankish Church across the Channel.

Augustine's Relationship with the King

Whatever his hopes and fears on arrival in Canterbury, Augustine had enjoyed rapid initial success. Several challenges had faced Augustine on arrival in Kent: gaining acceptance of the mission by the king and earning the trust and support of Queen Bertha who had requested the mission; establishing himself and his companions at Saint Martin's; gaining the confidence of Aethelberht and preparing him for baptism; building a cathedral and priory as the base for his mission and discerning the right approach to mission for the different sections of Kentish society among whom he would minister.

Until Augustine had sufficient fluency in Old English, Bertha would have acted as interpreter. She wrote and spoke Latin, so that right from the arrival of the missionaries at St Martin's Hill Bertha would be Augustine's go-between with King Aethelberht, particularly during the first anxious months while the king deliberated whether to receive Christian baptism. The queen's good will and active support for the new bishop were essential for any progress in an environment so different from Rome. Augustine, by arriving both as emissary of the pope and as a bishop recently consecrated by 'the bishops of the Germanies' in Francia, had opened the way for Bertha to accept him as her chaplain and confessor. What was critical for them both was to nudge the king towards baptism and open the door for mission in the fertile pagan soil of Saxon Kent.

Plans for a Cathedral and Abbey

At an early stage, possibly soon after Aethelberht's baptism, plans began to crystallize for two monastic communities – a cathedral supported by a priory within Canterbury as Augustine's see city; and an abbey outside the city wall, below Saint Martin's Chapel, to serve also as a mausoleum for Aethelberht's royal dynasty. The king gave freely of his own land and material resources to fund both enterprises. Together these would form an almost unbroken block of land stretching from St Martin's Hill into the former Roman city.

An area of ground was selected further west for the cathedral, on derelict ground within the northeast corner of the city wall. Christ Church Cathedral and Priory, the first new construction within the city walls for two centuries, became the centre of an active apostolate. The preaching that took place after Aethelberht's baptism and for the next few years would have been almost entirely by the Frankish contingent who spoke a dialect that could be understood by the *Angli*. What is significant is that the Anglo-Saxons first heard the preaching of the gospel through interpreters of the Frankish Church, whose bishops had themselves refused to respond to Bertha's call.[11]

Augustine was not resident in Christ Church Priory for long; the cathedral was only dedicated in June 602 or 603. Its name was taken from the façade of the Lateran Basilica in Rome: *Christo Salvatori*, Christ the Saviour. Like the Lateran Basilica, Christ Church Cathedral in Canterbury was not founded over the remains of an apostle or martyr; there was neither an earlier church beneath the foundations, nor any tomb of a Christian apostle or martyr over which to build. Augustine, however, did not wait until cathedral and abbey were completed before the mission among the English people began in earnest.

The substantial parcel of land that Aethelberht allocated for the abbey was roughly comparable to the area of Saint Andrew's Monastery in Rome. The abbey chapel lay on an east–west line with Saint Martin's Chapel. As a very clear signal to the people, Augustine is said to have exorcised a demon from Aethelberht's personal pagan shrine that stood on the abbey site. This spiritual contest left scorchmarks on the wall of the shrine, later dedicated as a small chapel. In the late seventh century the chapel was incorporated into the newly built Saint Pancras Church as its south portico.[12]

As work began on the cathedral a number of pressing issues also needed urgent resolution.

Augustine's Ecclesiastical Concerns

The unexciting and energy-sapping part of mission lies in the detail and, like Martin of Tours before him, Augustine could not escape the more mundane pressures of the office of bishop. Some arose from the mixed community at Saint Martin's Chapel and the liturgical needs of the Frankish priests who had accompanied Augustine to Kent. The demands of constant travel to distant parts of Aethelberht's kingdom, coupled with concerns over the building of the two Canterbury monasteries, juggling competing demands on his attention and petitioning Pope Gregory for more support, would have taken their toll.

To compound matters, Augustine was not well prepared for his role as bishop. He had not served as a secular priest under a diocesan bishop, and given the circumstance of his consecration in Francia, he is unlikely to have had much insight into the wider affairs of how to govern the Church. As Gregory had not initially considered consecrating Augustine as bishop, his briefing to Augustine on his return to Francia would lack some of the basics that other bishops could be expected to know. Subsequent events seem to confirm this, as Augustine's pastoral inquiry to Gregory shows.[13]

Augustine's letter to Gregory may have been written as early as 598 or as late as 601. The earlier date may be more realistic, as the missionaries' immediate social and ecclesiastical context in Canterbury forced certain urgent questions to the fore. Augustine's nine questions to Gregory were wide ranging, but it was not until 601 that Augustine received a reply. For four years Augustine would have to ad lib his responses to some of his most urgent questions, but Gregory had been heavily involved in peace negotiations in 599 between the Eastern Empire and the Lombards. His health, also, had been poor, and in June 600 he wrote that he had been unable to rise from his couch for longer than three hours, even for Mass or the principal festivals.

Augustine charged two of his Roman companions, Peter and Laurence, with taking his letter to Rome, but they were also key figures in the future of the mission. Peter became Abbot of Saint Peter and Saint Paul's Monastery outside the walls of Canterbury, and Augustine later appointed Laurence as his successor in Canterbury. This suggests the extremely difficult position that Augustine found himself in at this time, that he was willing to risk sending his two closest companions back through Francia to urgently petition Pope Gregory for reinforcements at the earliest possible moment.

During this period Augustine took on the task of laying out the ground plan for his new cathedral within the derelict city and supervised the building project. The missionaries continued to worship at Saint Martin's outside the walls for perhaps four years until the building of the cathedral was complete, possibly in 602 or 603. At the same time, the diverse needs of his mixed party, comprising monks, lay brothers, priests and lay clerks, had become pressing.

Augustine's first question to Gregory addresses this directly. Not all of the Franks who had accompanied Augustine to England were celibate priests – some were lay clerks, and some found wives from among the local community. How should Augustine deal with this?

Augustine would have noted the way that bishops shared a collegiate but not common life with their priests at Aix-en-Provence, Vienne, Lyon, Autun, Tours and possibly at other cathedrals en route. Gregory's advice to Augustine was that, as a monk first, he should live a full common life together with his monks. This would imply a monastic priory, possibly under the supervision of Laurentius in the role of prior. Few of the monks from Rome would have been ordained, other than Augustine and Laurentius. However, the Frankish clergy (or 'ordained clerks') may have lived a collegiate but not monastic life, after the Frankish cathedral pattern at Aix, Arles, Tours and elsewhere. Both groups would have been supported by the revenues accruing from gifts and tithes to the Church. The lay clerks 'who did not receive holy orders' would receive an income from the 'emoluments which accrue' to the Church and be permitted to marry.

Given the strong adherence of the Anglo-Saxons to their heathen shrines, how should Augustine respond to them as a missionary? Looking ahead to future ecumenical contacts, how should Augustine deal with the Frankish and the British bishops?

Alongside these were some very down-to-earth questions, relating to nocturnal emissions affecting a priest's fitness to celebrate the sacraments, who may marry whom, baptism, and when women could return to church after menstruation, 'because all these things the ignorant English people needed to know'. Strangely, Liudhard did not seem to have addressed these issues in the decades before 597, but perhaps this underlines the rapid increase in the membership of the Canterbury Christian community after Christmas 597.

Augustine seemed reluctant to turn to the Frankish priests for advice on how the more down-to-earth issues of pastoral practice should be handled. His questions are enormously revealing and indicate more than merely an anxious personality; he lacked the basic training that any secular priest in Rome would have expected to receive before exercising pastoral care and oversight of a parish church.

Mission and Message

There were two distinct audiences for the missionaries in heathen Kent: the king together with his noblemen and warriors and the large number of peasant farmers. For the warrior class, having yet another god was not in itself an issue, but the exclusivity of the Christian God was. Augustine knew, from his time at Tours acquainting himself with Saint Martin's life and works, what a slow business conversion of an ancient culture would be. A significant appeal for warriors would lie in the battles and victories of the kings and in the Old Testament 'warrior' Psalms, which spoke directly of God as a god of war, of heroism and reward, honour and glory, but also of sacrifice, death and resurrection, with the promise of the faithfulness of God to the end, assistance in battle in the present and the rewards of the Kingdom in the life hereafter.

In a pre-literate culture unable to understand books or pictures, the Gospel narrative had a powerful appeal across the whole of society. It meant at a very simple level the story of a child born miraculously of a virgin mother, born in the dead of winter, surrounded significantly by familiar beasts of the field, the ox and the ass, with the sheep and shepherds close by on a hillside on a frosty winter's night. It is the story of an infant whose birth was mystically connected with a time of peace over the whole earth and who grew to manhood, suffered a bloody wound and died to be resurrected again from the dead. Perhaps most importantly, the death and resurrection of Jesus was a necessity that the world might live.

For the peasants who farmed the land and harvested the sea, whose lives were made precarious by the vagaries of weather, famine and plague and for whom charms and spells seemed their only defence against disaster and death, the Gospel stories spoke directly to their experience. Jesus had gone about the countryside, speaking the farmers' language of seed and grain, the fishermen's language of nets and storms, and meeting human needs by casting out demons and healing the sick. These stories made an enormous impression among the ordinary people of

Kent and even more so when the missionaries began to confirm them with miracles of their own.

The new story, myth or religion was compatible with many fertility rites and observances among the Saxons such as the blessing of the plough, rivers and the sea and the conjuration (what a magician says in casting a spell) of fruit trees. The missionaries offered prayers for good seasons, rain for the general fertility of the earth, thanksgiving at harvest and mourning and rejoicing at Easter for the death of the god and his resurrection.[14]

What is certain is that, from the outset, this new story was told first from the lips of Frankish interpreters who spoke a dialect of the Anglo-Saxon tongue, rather than by the Roman monks who did not.

King and Countrymen: The Mission Grows

Augustine expanded the mission beyond the immediate confines of Canterbury by travelling with the king on his frequent visitations around his kingdom. However, preaching the gospel to the ruling classes did not fall only to Augustine. Within a few years Aethelberht had taken upon himself the role of evangelist in exercising his influence at a royal level for the baptism of the rulers of the neighbouring kingdoms in Essex and East Anglia.

The royal household travelled frequently by ship to their royal centres at a distance from Canterbury, providing Augustine with opportunities to meet and preach to nobles, warriors and farmers. 'During a royal visit, local people were required to perform traditional services, but in return the king became available to his people. He was there to settle disputes, administer justice and reward in front of witnesses those who served him well.'[15]

Aethelberht's kingdom was divided into blocks of land called lathes that provided communities with access to a range of territory and natural resources. These typically included coastal and estuary salt marshes, agricultural land and woodland, extensive pasture, open and woodland grazing, swine pastures, timber and, in later years, building-stone. All communities also had common access to the Weald, including those as distant as the Isle of Thanet. A common feature of Aethelberht's royal centres was a navigable river, a hilltop dominating the surrounding countryside or a place at the junction of a Roman road. Eastry (Eastring, indicating a royal hall) was one of these. It lies between Richborough and Dover on a prehistoric trackway that linked the *vill* to early Sandwic on the Wantsum estuary, and an inlet further south gave access to the coast. A royal hall or palace may have existed beneath the present manor house near the church.

To the west and northwest of Canterbury, towns such as Aylesford, Wye (*Weowara*), Faversham, Milton Regis, Rainham and Teynham were all developed as royal *vills* during the early Anglo-Saxon period. They are evenly spaced along the line of Roman-built Watling Street, between Richborough Fort and London, similar to the towns that dot the *Via Aurelia* in Provence. These provided ideal opportunities for missionary activity.

Conversion to Christ was one element in mission, but changing the culture and practices of a nation quite another. For some considerable time, the adoption of Christianity meant a significant degree of religious syncretism. Gregory responded with flexibility when it came to Augustine's dealings with the heathen customs of the Anglo-Saxons. Having already sent a letter to Augustine on how to deal with the customs of the heathens, Gregory had second thoughts. The pope's revised strategy was meant to address concerns that the king might be moving too far ahead of his people. Gregory suggested that the missionaries focus on the kernel of the faith, leaving the husk to perish as practices changed and faith matured.

On 17 June 601 Gregory sent fresh instructions to Abbot Mellitus, as he made his journey to England:

I have come to the conclusion that the temples of the idols in England should not on any account be destroyed. Augustine must smash the idols, but the temples themselves should be sprinkled with holy water and altars set up in them in which relics are to be enclosed . . . In this way I hope the people (seeing their temples are not destroyed) will leave their idolatry and yet continue to frequent the places as formerly, so coming to know and revere the true God.[16]

This would prove crucial among the rural inhabitants of Kent if there were to be any long-term future for the mission.

Mission among Peasant Farmers

Bede provides very little detail of Augustine's missionaries as they went out to people on their farms, in hamlets, at *wics* along the coast and riverbanks, travelling on foot and by boat to reach both populated areas and remote places. Several Roman roads spread out from Canterbury, providing access to the growing *wics* beyond the city on the River Stour as well as nearby agricultural hamlets at Littlebourne and Blean and the Wantsum Channel, ringed with fishing settlements at Fordwich, Sturry, Upstreet, Sarre, Minster, Wickhambreaux and Preston. All were easily accessible by boat, and the missionaries would have little difficulty reaching these settlements within a day by leaving at dawn and returning to Saint Martin's by nightfall. The missionaries travelled together for support and protection in a society where everyone carried at least a belt knife, and forests provided shelter for desperate outlaws.

Peasant farmers overwhelmingly formed the greater proportion of Aethelberht's kingdom, and the missionaries would have little difficulty finding them near to their timber and thatch *havels*. The mission would have little chance of lasting impact unless their needs, practical as well as spiritual, were met.

The monks and interpreters spoke to individuals and preached. In an uncertain and precarious world, everyone put their faith in something, and the monks' message was to put their faith in Christ as their saviour, rock and shelter. Bede, writing his account of Aidan's mission to Northumbria that followed three decades later, records that the monks always came with something to give to those whom they met, and never asked anything for themselves. This was in marked contrast to their overlords and warriors who took whatever they wanted.

A first meeting could lead to a second, preaching Good News and offering prayers to members of the families living in a village or hamlet; then another until the community came to receive baptism, following in the steps of their king. Finally, the local shrine would be consecrated for Christian worship and the pagan contents exchanged for Christian symbols and furnishings. This approach slowly built resilient local Christian communities, supported by monasteries that began to spread along the river inlets, coastlands and islands – Thanet, Richborough, Sheppey, Dover and the Saxon Shore.

For the sick and suffering, the missionaries prayed and treated wounds and ailments with ointments and medicines. The hamlets and market places that ringed the Wantsum Channel and Kent coast also gave the missionaries an insight into the short, disease-ridden and desperate lives of ordinary people in sixth-century England. To cope with misfortunes on a day-to-day level certain practices, such as burning barley in a house where there had been a death to protect the living, continued until late in the seventh century. The auroch, boar and snake were believed to possess magic powers, and some wells, trees and stones were held sacred. Fertility rites were a common practice, and traces of this persisted in the worship of the earth goddess Nerthus by a group of German tribes, including the Angles and Jutes.[17]

Mortality in childbirth was high. Every village had its own small knot of orphans, and most first-time mothers would face childbirth without the support of their own mothers at their bedside.[18] A belief in the afterlife was common, as burials in chamber graves with grave-goods suggest, but there is no clear indication what this belief meant, except that the immortality all English warriors hoped for was in the memory of their prowess in battle. 'It was a religion almost devoid of theology, but abounding in taboos, charms and magical incantations, designed to ward-off evil or ensure success in this life, with little thought beyond. The immortality sought by the heathen English was in the remembrance of heroic deeds.'[19] Peasant families hoped that the few treasured possessions, which had accompanied them in life, would also comfort them in death.

The missionaries would also have looked for opportunities to redeem slaves and include them as freedmen in their monastic community, as Pope Gregory had done. The practice of not coercing religious obedience (Rome's usual method) on the one hand, and of giving away rather than taking for themselves, forged a deep-rooted faith among peasant farming communities able to withstand the brief periods of apostasy that took place within a decade across Kent and in London.

Within less than a century the monasteries had achieved the enormous task of transforming the lives and culture of several Saxon tribes that would one day constitute the English nation. What the missionaries brought was not only a message of spiritual salvation, but also practical skills and new technologies that were unknown among sixth-century English farmers. The monks' skills in both agriculture and horticulture brought new practices and technology from both Rome and the Frankish kingdoms. Within a generation methods of growing agricultural produce changed through the introduction of paddocks, fences, enclosures, trackways, banks and ditches to define the fields.

The agricultural knowledge of the monks made more intensive farming possible by using heavier ploughs drawn by teams of eight oxen. Greater productivity led to the growth of local markets, followed by networks of roads and pathways. Trade was made easier through silver coins minted at Canterbury, and surplus wealth brought peasant farmers into contact with the international *wics* that had sprung up in the Wantsum, river inlets and on the Kent coast. Even the *Angli* of modest means were drawn into international trade through purchases of glassware, cups, pottery and woven cloth from Continental emporia.

Mission and Miracle

A sanatorium would have been a necessary part of Augustine's living arrangements near Saint Martin's Chapel, with urgent priority given to a herb garden for medicines and ointments. From the outset the monks' ministry of healing would be administered through the traditional means of ointments and medicines at the same time that the building work on the churches began in Canterbury.

In Bede's writings material relating to signs and wonders was accepted as wholly appropriate to a historical narrative. He brought together the history and hagiography of holy men and women to show how God had worked out his purposes for the world through particular people.[20] However, in this instance Bede's record of Gregory's pastoral response to Augustine has unfortunately obscured a notable ministry of healing and miracle that took place through Augustine and his monks, and that these wonders, healing in diseased and broken bodies as well as souls, were an authentic witness to the gospel for their time.

Gregory, in a letter to Eulogius, Patriarch of Alexandria, in July 598, wrote that more than 10,000 of the *Angli* had been baptized the previous Christmas and that Augustine 'and those that have been sent with him are *resplendent with such great miracles in the said nation that they seem to imitate the powers of the apostles* in the signs which they display'.[21] The mass baptism that Gregory refers to took place in December 597 in the context of religious rites celebrating the changing year, a time when sacrificial animals were eaten at ritual feasts.

The most sacred pagan festival was the winter solstice, Modranicht (Mother Night) on 21 or 22 December, as it ushered in the New Year. The 25 December was also a pagan festival, and the symbolism of old beliefs given new meaning would be too much to let slip by. Gregory wrote approvingly that both Augustine and his monks participated in a ministry of 'powers' and 'miracles' on this occasion and on others.

Bede mentions miracles in regard to Augustine's ministry more frequently than for any other saint except Saint Cuthbert. In 603 or 604 Augustine performed a healing miracle while meeting with the British bishops by restoring the sight of a young Saxon man when the British bishops were unable to do so. However, it is clear that Gregory's concern was not for the miracles but their impact on Augustine himself. In a letter in 601 Gregory strongly warned Augustine that the purpose of outward miracles is to draw people to inward grace. The pope's new Bishop of Canterbury needed to be careful that 'the weak mind' was not raised up by a self-esteem that could lead to an inward 'fall'. Not all the elect performed miracles, but all have their names recorded in heaven. Gregory reminds Augustine to note carefully that he belongs to Christ; he is not his own master.[22]

Pope Gregory was undoubtedly correct to encourage Augustine not to be carried away by performing miracles but instead to count the high spiritual cost that such a ministry places on the one who exercises it. This is a caution he could well have given to any miracle-working saint of this period. However, the unfortunate outcome for Augustine is that history has not remembered the English mission because of the missionaries' miraculous works, but rather that the first archbishop was reproved by the pope for the potential effect that miracles could have upon his soul. Consequently, almost no credit has attached to Augustine – or his companions – for the evidently significant part that miracles played in bringing the Anglo-Saxons to faith.

Reminiscent of Martin of Tours, the fruit of Augustine's miracles came long after the end of his life on the mission field. A century after the landing in 597, an Anglo-Saxon chapel was dedicated to Augustine within Richborough Fort. Abbot Bassa built a similar chapel for his monastery at Reculver in 669, and he may have supervised the religious communities that attached to both.

Thorne, a fourteenth-century monk in Canterbury, recorded that a stone on which Augustine had trod as he disembarked at Richborough had retained the imprint of the saint's foot. This stone was later preserved in Augustine's chapel within the old fort. Each year, on the anniversary of the stone's deposit in the chapel, crowds of people gathered to pray for the recovery of their health. Popular belief about the sanctity of the chapel was widespread, and those who were ill and suffering found their way there in significant numbers. The chapel continued to be used for worship in this way as late as the seventeenth century.[23]

We can only surmise what Pope Gregory might have made of that.

Notes

1   Gregory the Great, Book XI, Letter 29.
2   Bede, *Ecclesiastical History* I.26.
3   Rowan Williams, 'Monks and Mission: A perspective from England', 2012, www.archbishopofcanterbury.org/articles. php?action=search&tag_id=6&tag_id=6&tag_id=6&tag_id=6&tag_id=6&sort=date&order=desc&page=2.
4   Bede, *Ecclesiastical History* I.26.
5   Richard Gameson (ed.), *St Augustine and the Conversion of England*, Stroud: Sutton Publishing Ltd, 1999, p. 19.
6   Stephane Lebecq, 'England and the Continent in the Sixth and Seventh Centuries: The Question of Logistics', in Gameson, *St Augustine*, p. 56.
7   Stuart Brookes and Sue Harrington, *The Kingdom and People of Kent, AD 400–1066*, Stroud: History Press, 2010, p. 94.
8   Nicholas Brooks, *The Early History of the Church of Canterbury: Christ Church from 597 to 1066*, London and New York: Leicester University Press, 1984, p. 9.
9   Bede, *Ecclesiastical History* I.26.
10 Bede, *Ecclesiastical History* I.26.
11 Richard Gem (ed.), *St Augustine's Abbey Canterbury*, London: B. T. Batsford, 1997, p. 20.
12 Rev. Canon Routledge, 'Roman Foundations at St Pancras, Canterbury', *Archaeologia Cantiana* 14 (1892), p. 103.
13 Bede, *Ecclesiastical History* I.27.
14 Brian Branston, *The Lost Gods of England*, London: Thames & Hudson, 1974, p. 55.
15 John H. Williams (ed.), *The Archaeology of Kent to AD 800*, Kent History Project 8, Woodbridge: The Boydell Press and Kent County Council, 2007, p. 243.
16 Bede, *Ecclesiastical History* I.30.
17 K. P. Witney, *The Kingdom of Kent*, London: Phillimore, 1982, p. 112.

18 Robin Fleming, *Britain after Rome: The Fall and Rise 400–
   1070*, London: Allen Lane (Penguin), 2010, p. 365.
19 Witney, *Kingdom of Kent*, p. 113.
20 Alan Thacker, 'Bede and History', in Scott DeGregorio (ed.),
   The Cambridge Companion to Bede, Cambridge: Cambridge
   University Press, 2010, p. 170.
21 Gregory the Great, Book VII, Letter 40.
22 Bede, *Ecclesiastical History* II.31.
23 C. R. Smith, *The Antiquities of Richborough, Reculver and
   Lympne, in Kent*, London: John Russell Smith, 1850, p. 160.

10

Augustine and the British Church

Augustine's failure to win over the British Church is mostly remembered as the darkest moment for the English mission. The consequences were disastrous for all parties involved in the negotiations that took place between Augustine and the leaders of the British Church and incalculable for the future course of mission in the centuries that followed. This encounter also raises questions concerning the extent of Gregory's own influence on the course of events and the consequences for King Aethelberht and the kingdom of Kent.

Compared to his answers to Augustine on local pastoral matters in 601, Gregory's responses to wider ecumenical relationships were brief in the extreme. Augustine's sixth question was how should he deal with the bishops of Gaul and Britain respectively? Gregory sympathized with Augustine that Frankish bishops visited England so seldom as to make their participation impractical in a fast-growing church. However, it was not part of Gregory's consideration that the British bishops might assist in consecrations or even join in a united mission to the Anglo-Saxons. That was an initiative Augustine took in consultation with King Aethelberht. Bede briefly records that Gregory committed to Augustine:

All the bishops of Britain that the unlearned may be instructed, the weak strengthened by your counsel [an implicit reference to the British Church following a different method for dating Easter], and the perverse [possibly a reference to adherence to Pelagian heresy] corrected by your authority.[1]

In this the pope showed a significant blind spot in a letter that is otherwise astute and sensitive to local English practices. While Gregory recognized the ancient authority and autonomy of the Frankish Archbishop of Arles and other Frankish bishops, he offered no such concession to the British bishops. As some of these had been, and others might still be, adherents to the teachings of Pelagius, the pope regarded the bishops as heretics in a Christendom now firmly committed to the teachings of Augustine of Hippo.

In another letter Gregory's intentions are made a little clearer: Augustine should subject under himself:

> not only those whom you ordain, and those whom the bishop of York may ordain, but also all the priests of Britain, so that they may learn the form of right belief and good living from the conversation and life of your Holiness, and, executing their office well in their faith and life, may attain to heavenly kingdoms when it may please the Lord.[2]

King Aethelberht's Involvement

A journey to the border of British territory could not be undertaken without significant support from Aethelberht. What attracted the king to Augustine's venture with the British bishops, particularly as Aethelberht had little interest in continuing a Saxon onslaught on British territories? The kingdom of Kent had played only a minor role in the historic battle of Badon Hill (*Mons Badonicus*) and was little affected by the outcome. The battle may have taken place during 490–517, a major military event that shaped the political landscape of post-Roman Britain in favour of the British for more than a century.

However, for Aethelberht the concept of a supreme peacekeeper and mediator fitted well with his role as *bretwalda* (honorary Saxon overlord). The prospect of a *Christian* England, proselytized from Kent, and maintaining a special patronage over the British kingdoms, may have held much promise for new values that still left a place for the old. The idea of a British Church working under the guidance of an archbishop whose patron was the King of Kent in the conversion of the other English kingdoms was a bold conception, but could it be achieved?

Augustine's Journey to Meet with the British Church

For the expedition to the West, Augustine's party probably included Mellitus, soon but briefly to become Bishop of London, Justus and also Laurentius, but most significantly King Aethelberht and his *gesiths*, whose warriors they gathered en route from Reculver, Sheppey and the Medway. Aethelberht's overlordship of Essex would partly ensure safe passage through the Thames Estuary and beyond London.

The distance by boat from Reculver to the source of the Thames in Gloucestershire is approximately 250 miles. The tidal Thames ceases at Teddington Lock, which is 14 feet (4.3 m) above sea level. A further 44 locks lie between Teddington and Thameshead, rising by 346 feet, so that the greater part of the river journey would have been on foot. The total distance is comparable to Augustine's river journey of 270 miles from Arles in Provence to Chalon-sur-Saône in Burgundy. In every other respect, however, this was a very different journey.

There was little commercial traffic on the Thames compared to the Rhône; no barges, horses, oxen or paths along the riverbanks and no overnight *mansios* to welcome travellers. In reality, very few if any travellers would have attempted a journey through hostile tribes to the source of the great river. During the days of Roman administration Britannia could be regarded as a punishment posting. On this occasion some four centuries later Augustine and his companions would be travelling through potentially hostile territory with the very barbarians they had formerly so greatly feared; but even for the Kent Saxons, this would be no easy journey to the source of England's own 'heart of darkness'.

The journey may have provided the recently arrived Mellitus with first sight of a potential cathedral location for his new 'see city'. What the party found on the north bank of the Thames was a Saxon trading station, Lundenwic, consisting of little more than a thousand people who lived west of the River Fleet. To the east of the Fleet lay the ruins of the former Roman city of Londinium, later renamed Lundenburh by the West Saxons. By 604 the Roman era cathedral no longer existed, and Mellitus was compelled to establish a new site. Its location remains uncertain, possibly somewhere beneath Fenchurch Street.

Bede records that Mellitus's cathedral was located in Lundenwic, which would seem an obvious place among the population, but there is no evidence for this. Rather it was the practice of the period to build a cathedral, as Augustine had in Canterbury, within the walls of former Roman towns. Mellitus it seems chose Ludgate Hill in Lundenburh, building over the ruins of a former Roman temple dedicated to Diana.

Pope Gregory's original intention was to re-establish London as the seat of an archbishop in the south of England and to have another archbishop at York in the north. However, Aethelberht's nephew King Saeberht had yet to commit himself to the Christian faith and receive baptism. His hospitality to the party as they journeyed upriver would have been generous nonetheless.

Augustine's Oak – Meeting Place with the British Bishops

With King Aethelberht's assistance, Augustine summoned the bishops and teachers of the neighbouring British kingdoms to a conference. Their first exploratory meeting was held in c. 603. Aethelberht is not mentioned directly by Bede in his account of this episode (recorded in *Ecclesiastical History* II.2), but the king's presence would be crucial to any agreement that Augustine hoped to achieve.

The areas from which the representatives of the British Church came could have extended as far as Somerset in the southwest and Wales and Chester in the northwest, areas in which significant concentrations of British rulers, bishops and monasteries were located in western Britain. According to Bede, the first Archbishop of Canterbury met with representatives of the British Church, called by Bede *episcopos sive doctores*, bishops or teachers, many from the Welsh monastery of Bangor Iscoed.

The meeting is said to have taken place at 'Augustine's Oak' somewhere on the borders of the *Hwicce* and West Saxons, in the area of present-day Gloucestershire.[3] Such a meeting place, in Kemble forest near to Thameshead, a spring that feeds the headwaters of the Thames some 360 feet (110 m) above sea level, would have been a convenient location for gathering representatives from sub-Roman locations such as St Deiniol's Monastery in Bangor (established c. 560) and Saint Illtud's Monastery at Cor Tewdws (present-day Llantwit Major in South Wales), but also from Cadbury-Congresbury and Saint Congar's Monasteries, both in Somerset.

Augustine's First Meeting with Rulers of the British Church

Augustine, taking his cue from Pope Gregory and making use of his influence with Aethelberht, 'summoned' the bishops and teachers of the neighbouring kingdom to a conference somewhere west of the Cotswolds. For once Augustine would not need a translator, as the conversation would be conducted in Latin, still the language of the British Church. Aethelberht would be at a linguistic disadvantage, needing to rely on Augustine's resources to both translate and interpret events as the meeting unfolded.

In Bede's account, Augustine urged them with 'brotherly admonitions' to preserve the catholic peace. When negotiations did not go smoothly, Augustine finally 'rebuked' the bishops. In reality, Gregory could not have given Augustine authority over an ancient and autonomous British Church without their willing consent. However, the words that Bede ascribes to Augustine do not carry a sense of disapproval – Bede had little regard for the British Church, if not contempt. In his view it deserved what ultimately followed and cleared the way for a Christian 'English nation'.

The divisive issue between the British and Roman Churches was the date of Easter (as it would be later with the Irish monks of Lindisfarne at the Synod of Whitby in 664). The date of Easter was not a trivial issue. If the Roman and British missions were to run side by side, converts should not be confused over two competing festivals to celebrate the most significant event of their new lives, their Easter baptism. To do so would not only lead to conflict between the baptized, it would render a unified English mission impossible from the outset.

After hours of unfruitful dispute, Bede records that: 'the holy father Augustine drew the meeting to a close and, to vouchsafe his bona fides, said: Let some sick man be brought, and let the faith and practice of him by whose prayers he is healed be considered as in accordance with God's will and proper for us all to follow.'[4] This was not well received by the British contingent who reluctantly agreed, and a blind Saxon was brought forward. The British bishops prayed for him, but no benefit was visible from their ministry. Then Augustine, 'compelled by genuine necessity', as we might well imagine, prayed, and the man's sight was restored. Everyone acknowledged that Augustine was a true herald, but although they recognized that Augustine preached the true way of righteousness, they could not disown their former customs without the approval of their bishops and rulers.

The first conference ended without resolution, but with an agreement to meet again and with more people in attendance. The presence of an Anglo-Saxon king with his warrior-entourage had probably contributed little to creating the right atmosphere for successful negotiations. The differences in height and physical presence between the king's warriors and the British contingent would have been striking and intimidating. Although archaeological data from cemeteries indicates the average height of Anglo-Saxon men was a little over 5 feet 8 inches compared to an estimate of just under 5 feet 7 inches for British males,[5] Aethelberht's men were not chosen for their average height.

The Second Conference

The venue of the second meeting may again have been at Augustine's Oak, but other venues have variously been suggested: somewhere on the border between England and Wales; Abbersley in Worcestershire, or alternatively near Bangor Iscoed Monastery in Wales. Bangor would be a longer and even more arduous journey for Augustine than his first. For this meeting seven British bishops and many learned men came, chiefly from Bangor (*Bancornaburg*) under the rule of Abbot Dinoot. Other bishops may have come from further afield than Bangor, including Worcester, which possibly had its own bishop, and Somerset, where bishops and rulers may have attended from west of the River Axe, the boundary between the West Saxons and the British. Between the first and second meetings local rulers and kings must also have been consulted. If representatives from areas as widespread as these were present at the meeting with Augustine, the complexity of their ensuing negotiations becomes evident.

Forging a lasting political peace, brokered with the various Saxon groupings and accepting the Roman Church's archiepiscopal oversight in the western parts of sub-Roman Britain, would require the conclusion of a formal treaty underwritten by Aethelberht. Such agreement could not have been reached unless a significant body of British opinion was willing to accept it. Such an agreement would only be reached through the active diplomacy of lay and clerical leaders – Augustine and Aethelberht, the British rulers, their bishops and the abbots. However, the absence of a recognized government for the British contingent, with one voice capable of speaking authoritatively for the diversity of British interests at the two meetings, was a serious handicap that underscored the fragility of peace in the kingdoms in the west.

The basis of agreement would need to lie in some commonality of interest. Gregory's main purpose, working through Augustine, was to overcome what he believed to be heresy concerning the date of Easter and to bring the British Church under the influence of Rome. Such a vision made little headway among the diverse body of clerics, who needed the clear direction that only a single government could provide, but this was not an option that seems to have been possible at that time.

The second meeting ended badly. From the outset the tone was fractious. Bede records, approvingly, that Augustine, following the lead from Gregory and also the counsel of his companions, failed to rise to his feet at the approach of the British bishops. Based on the advice of a hermit, the British party had watched for a sign: whether or not Augustine rose to greet them. On this evidence they concluded that Augustine was 'harsh and proud', not a man of God, and so they had no need to submit to his words.

Bede's overall account of the two conferences was meant to convey that Augustine, the missionary from Rome, possessed mystical powers of healing and prophecy and an innate gravitas. However, the two ecclesiastical cultures were different. Whereas the Roman Church emphasized the dignity of the office of bishop, the British outlook was rather that Christian authority rested less in an office than in the quality of humility in following in the footsteps of Christ, the servant of all.[6]

Despite the synthesis of these two models that Augustine had been able to weave together in Canterbury, he was not able to do so on British soil.

Augustine's Demands

Augustine was adamant that the British Church should accede to three demands: to keep Easter at the 'proper' time, to perform the sacrament of baptism according to Roman rites and to preach the word of the Lord to the English people in fellowship with Augustine's mission. In exchange Augustine would agree to 'tolerate' everything else the British Church did that was seen as an offence to sixth-century Roman orthodoxy.

In Augustine's two encounters with the British Church, there may have been additional factors that also rendered the prospect of agreement unlikely from the outset, forces that lay beneath the surface of their differences in doctrine and practice. The social structure of British Christians in the early seventh century may itself have played a dominant if not a determining role, and a more significant factor even than ecclesiastical differences such as the date of Easter may have been the low moral state of the British Church itself.[7]

Behind the bishops of the British Church stood the rulers of several small kingdoms, exerting an invisible but real influence over the outcome of proceedings. The bishops were not only dependent on them for protection, they were also kith and kin from the same families, sharing a common ancestry and faith. From the British perspective, it was not only their religious identity that was at stake, but also their political independence. An association with Augustine and Aethelberht might not have been seen as either essential or desirable for the future of British Christianity, nor for the political organization and prosperity of the British kingdoms in the West of the country.

Augustine was looking for submission to Rome, and Aethelberht would be looking for a treaty that stabilized political relationships between his kingdom and the British territories. For the British an association with Rome carried the drawback of submission and obligations that met the aspirations neither of the British rulers nor of their bishops.

It is also seems that trade and ecclesiastical links with the Eastern Roman Empire were being cultivated by Constantinople, perhaps part of a strategy of patronage and influence, so that for the British contingent, links with Canterbury would seem much less attractive. The British Church had a long monastic history, a characteristic that it shared with the Eastern Empire, whereas the Roman Church was a relative newcomer to monasticism and had little to offer the British Church in terms of biblical scholarship or monastic discipline.

However, what Augustine could offer was a way back to a relationship with the world of Continental Christianity and a treaty of co-operation and protection from the gathering storm coming from the West Saxons and Northumbrians. The British had won at Badon Hill a century before and more recently had held the West Saxons at the River Axe in Somerset, giving a false confidence that they could successfully defend themselves from further invasion.

Whatever factors weighed the heaviest in their deliberations, the British delegation rejected outright Augustine's three demands: to keep Easter at the proper time, to use the baptism rites of the holy Roman and apostolic Church and, in fellowship with Augustine, to preach the gospel to the English. Regarding the first two, Augustine had no room to manoeuvre: the date of Easter was critical for any work of evangelism they might undertake together, while the issue of heresy had long been settled in favour of Augustine of Hippo and against Pelagius. The third demand was itself dependent on the first two and could not stand alone.

Aftermath

Augustine warned the British contingent of the likely outcome of their rejection of this offer: if they refused to accept peace from their friends (Aethelberht and his English kingdom) they would have to accept war from their Anglo-Saxon enemies; and if they failed to preach and convert 'the English nation', the long-term consequences would be further bloodshed at the hands of heathen peoples.

Bede records, immediately after Augustine's closing words to the British, that a decade or so later (in 613 or 616) the full fury of the Saxons fell upon the British forces at Chester (*Caerlegion*) and the pagan Northumbrian king Aethelfrith slaughtered Bangor monks as they prayed for British victory on the battlefield. Augustine did not live to see this outcome. In the way Bede brings these two accounts together, Augustine's words to the

British bishops have inevitably been understood as a curse that brought on the Saxon attack.

The long journey, possibly repeated for the second conference, combined with the disappointing outcome of the meetings, seems to have broken Augustine's health. He returned to Canterbury, consecrated his successors Laurentius, Justus and Mellitus and died soon after. The long-term consequences of the encounter with the British Church were even more disastrous for Aethelberht. The Church would recover, but Aethelberht would not, nor would his kingdom, which had passed its zenith. His credibility and authority as *bretwalda* over the English kingdoms were fatally wounded by the public rebuff at the hands of the despised British. 'He was now entering upon old age and had no longer the resilience to recover from such a humiliation.'[8]

Aethelberht found himself in a similar position to the Bishop of Lyon, who held the title of 'Primate of All Gaul' but possessed little power. There was no one of Aethelberht's stature to replace him and ultimately no one of his character and competence to succeed him.

The Challenges of Conducting Mission Together

With the hindsight of 1400 years, the political cross-currents that lay beneath the surface of the two conferences may have been as influential if not more so than the ecclesiastical issues surrounding the date of Easter or the supremacy of the Bishop of Rome. The British Church leaders who met with Augustine initially appeared willing to co-operate in the huge task of converting the Anglo-Saxons, provided they were treated as valued partners in a common cause, rather than subordinates to an imposed, metropolitan authority.

However, the pope took little or no account of the ecumenical dimension of an English mission, omitted to address the leaders of the British Church directly (as a letter would have done) and failed to envision a framework that would have been acceptable to British interests as well as to Augustine and the Kentish king. It might have been possible at the time to find a place for the Anglo-Saxons as well as the British within an *ecclesia Britannica*,[9] but in reality the prize of a joint mission was not attractive enough, the bitterness between them too deep and the political support among the British kingdoms not forthcoming to create a common mission and a united Church. It has taken more than 1497 years for the first Welsh bishop to be appointed as Archbishop of Canterbury.

Augustine: An Evaluation

Within little more than two decades of Augustine's departure from Rome in 596, all the early founders of the English Church had passed away. Gregory died on 12 March 604, Augustine at some time between 604 and 610 (officially 26 May 604), Bertha in 612 and Aethelberht in 616. Peter, first abbot of the Abbey of Saint Peter and Saint Paul, died at sea off the coast of Francia after 613 and Laurence, who succeeded Augustine, died in 619. Augustine's mission to the *Angli* spanned 14 years at most and possibly as few as eight. The year of Augustine's death is not precisely known; informed opinion ranges from 604 to 610. The earlier date has been adopted throughout this book.

The judgement of historians on these years has not been unreservedly kind.[10] However, serving far from home, in a country whose customs and language were very different from his own, Augustine initiated the process of converting the Anglo-Saxons to Christianity, a watershed in the history of England, not only Kent, and whose consequences are felt to the present time. Augustine's simple lifestyle and hours of fervent prayer in Saint Martin's Chapel laid lasting foundations. The first Bishop of Canterbury left behind neither an account of the mission, nor a manuscript concerning his mission strategy, and only one letter is attributed to him.

Augustine initiated a pastoral mission that still characterizes the Church he came to establish in England. Canterbury's first archbishop laid the foundations for a generous Anglican orthodoxy and innovative liturgy that drew on the best of the worship practices available to him. Through building the abbey Augustine opened the way for scholarship that Hadrian and Theodore were later to build upon and created a mission that remained tolerant and sensitive to the pace of change Anglo-Saxon converts were able to sustain.

In the political sphere, Augustine brought the skills of writing to record and preserve Anglo-Saxon law codes that ensured personal rights and regulated actions, particularly the crucial aspect of the sale, transfer and inheritance of land. The relationship between monarch and people and Church and State, the establishment of rights and obligations and a civil service all have their roots in the first years following Augustine's arrival in Kent.

Augustine clearly demonstrated independent thinking and judgement as he developed his own mission strategy, and his actions were far more than a tactical adaptation of Gregory's ideas to an Anglo-Saxon context; there were too many gaps in the pope's plans to do otherwise. Augustine was willing to ask for insight and counsel in new situations where he had no experience, and it would be a curious understanding of leadership to regard this as a sign of weakness. He transcended his lack of experience as bishop and diplomat in his dealings with the royal courts of Francia and the kingdom of Kent. Augustine's initial relationship with his own priory, in living among his monks and the secular Frankish cathedral clergy, was different from Gregory's own arrangements in the Lateran Basilica and those pertaining in Frankish cathedrals. This arrangement was unique to Canterbury and would later become the norm in English cathedrals.

Augustine's relationship with the community of the still-forming Abbey of Saint Peter and Saint Paul reflected Gregory's relationship to Saint Andrew's Monastery in Rome, but he also recognized that King Aethelberht's desire for a royal burial chapel was a significant opportunity to bring his Latin-speaking Roman monks into the forefront of the mission.

The scope of Augustine's venture underwent changes during the course of his journey from Rome to Canterbury. Very little of this was anticipated at the outset. What had begun as a relatively low-level mission to provide support for Bertha at the Kentish royal court rapidly grew into very much more: a means to strengthen ties with Frankish rulers and reform the Frankish Church, involving it in the mission to England; to provide for the needs of a growing Christian community in the context of a new mission, develop close relationships with King Aethelberht and his court, appoint bishops and create new ecclesiastical structures in England, and bring the British Church in the West under the authority of Rome. Only in the latter could Augustine realistically be said to have fallen short of the expectations that the pope had placed upon him as he departed from Rome for the second and final time.

Augustine's Influence with Aethelberht

Augustine's arrival in 597 came at a crucial time for Aethelberht. The king was both fair-minded and generous to the missionaries. He was also concerned with his place in history, and Bertha's great ancestor Clovis I served as his model. Clovis was the first Christian king of the Franks, the first to issue a written law code, the first to establish his capital city in Paris and the first to be buried in a church. With Augustine's assistance Aethelberht replicated each of these achievements in Canterbury. In 604 he was the first Christian king of the Anglo-Saxons, the first to draw up a law code with the aid of the missionaries and the first among his Saxon peers to associate his royal seat with an ancient Romano-British city.

Augustine's aim as archbishop was to spread the gospel and build up the authority of the Church, particularly in his relationships with the temporal powers of the king. The gradual shaping of a single nation from diverse tribes of Anglo-Saxons, and the weaving together of a common tongue and a common faith, finally made possible the emergence of a monarch of a wholly modern ability in Alfred the Great. However, the tensions between a king's role in practical politics and the demands of being a servant of the Church could not easily be reconciled, as the deaths of two later archbishops – Thomas Becket and Cardinal Wolsey – would show.

In Canterbury Augustine's growing episcopal leadership involved him in an ever-widening range of activities: organizing and financing both episcopal and monastic households and protecting the young Church against violence and depredations. In minimizing attacks for plunder and pillage, Canterbury's location several miles inland from the coast was a decided advantage, but not a final barrier against Danish attacks. Augustine was also involved in devising the liturgy of the emerging English Church, defining Canterbury's relations as an episcopal see with its Frankish neighbours and working out the practical implications of the Church's beliefs for the daily lives of ordinary people.[11]

Aethelberht is the first clearly attested English king. Under him Kent emerges for the first time as a fully formed kingdom displaying many of the embryonic characteristics of later medieval states – law codes, a political and economic apparatus, a royal house and military capability. Inevitably, proximity to the royal court meant that the cathedral priory came to serve some of the needs of the newly converted Christian king; in particular Augustine's assistance to Aethelberht in framing his law code.

Davies describes a Burgundian Law Code similar to Aethelberht's, but promulgated nearly a century earlier:

> The Burgundian Code (or codes), which survives in thirteen extant manuscripts, is typical of the period when the Germanic peoples were adopting Christianity, entering literacy and codifying law . . . Mainly promulgated at Lugdunum by Gundobad [before 513], and revised under Sigismund, they

cover a huge range of subjects, starting with Gifts, Murders, and the emancipation of Slaves and finishing with Vineyards, Asses and Oxen taken in pledge.[12]

Unlike Gundobad's Frankish code, Latin, the language of the Church, would not be the official language of the State; Aethelberht chose to draft his law code in Old English. Augustine was not the author of new and coercive patterns of political expression that had already begun to emerge before the arrival of the missionaries, through new connections made possible with a wider Mediterranean world. From around 600, new patterns of taxation, law enforcement and imposed leadership began to find expression in an early form of Anglo-Saxon imperialism.[13] The emergence of trading emporia or *wics*, under the control of the Crown, along the Stour River and Wantsum Channel (Sarre, Fordwich, and later Sandwich and Wickhambreaux) reinforces this perception, and together with the reintroduction of coins minted in Kent may have begun under Aethelberht.

The semblance of an Anglo-Saxon 'civil service' and Registry for the Crown did not emerge for a further three centuries, after Alfred the Great captured London in 886. The impetus came from Alfred who, as writer and scholar, also arranged for the translation of the most crucial texts of the nation's Christian heritage from Latin into the vernacular. As this was primarily for the improvement of the clergy, in three centuries the wheel had turned 180 degrees.

In his relationship with Aethelberht, Augustine provided more than spiritual oversight of the royal court; he acted as mentor to the king. Gregory's letter to Aethelberht urged the king to receive counsel from Augustine and to take him into his confidence.[14] Later Justus, formerly Bishop of Rochester, on succeeding Mellitus as archbishop, performed the same role for King Eadbald.[15]

The relationships and exchanges between Gregory, Augustine and Aethelberht – conversations, suggestions, instructions, assistance, expressions of concern (and also flattery) – created a climate of trust that made possible the formulation of not only an

English legal system but the English character itself: an ability to compromise, the ability to see the other point of view and the belief that even pragmatism can serve the purposes of God.

As an able administrator, Augustine may have foreseen what he believed to be a necessary quality in the structure of the Church. On the one hand was the need for the mystical function of communion with God. On the other, the Church had to interpret the results of this communion and give them a political authority in the world of human affairs. The great problem has always been how to allocate these two functions, for it appears impossible for one man to be both an exploratory mystic and a practical statesman.[16]

This was precisely the tension Gregory experienced in holding to a monastic way of life while attending to the affairs of the Roman Church and State. The abbey and priory in Canterbury were instrumental in forming the spiritual and cultural values of the whole English Church. Augustine's mission demonstrated that both monastery and cathedral had an integral role within society, rather than outside of it.

A Broader Canvas

On the wider stage, the interplay between the Roman and the Christian 'civilized' world and barbarians (those who lived outside of civic society) was the essence of the so-called 'Dark Ages' in England (449–597). There are underlying patterns in the ways in which these two worlds interacted over time as the barbarians (Goths, Saxons, Vikings) made their permanent settlements inside the 'civilized' world. Barbarian invaders were slowly transformed from outsiders and assimilated first into the Roman Empire and second into the Christian faith. Barbarian cultures were dramatically changed by their encounters with 'civilization', but so too the Roman Empire was radically altered by their incorporation.

In the regions further north, beyond the reach of the Empire or the Roman Church, the emergence of national kings in

Scandinavia would occur largely under the auspices of the Church. The barbarian societies of the post-Roman world were to provide the soil from which these present nation-states derived.[17] In this process, Augustine's role in shaping the future course of Anglo-Saxon England was pivotal.

Notes

1 Bede, *Ecclesiastical History* I.27, VIII.
2 Gregory the Great, Book XI, Letter 65 to Augustine, Bishop of the *Angli*.
3 Richard Gameson (ed.), *St Augustine and the Conversion of England*, Stroud: Sutton Publishing Ltd, 1999, p. 35; Bruce Eagles, 'Augustine's Oak', *Medieval Archaeology* 47 (2003), p. 178.
4 Bede, *Ecclesiastical History* II.2.
5 Caroline Alexander, *Lost Gold of the Dark Ages: War, Treasure, and the Mystery of the Saxons*, New York: National Geographic Society, 2011, p. 54.
6 Gameson, *St Augustine*, p. 36.
7 Kenneth Hylson-Smith, *Christianity in England from Roman Times to the Reformation, Vol. I – From Roman Times to 1066*, London: SCM Press, 1999, p. 132.
8 K. P. Witney, *The Kingdom of Kent*, London: Phillimore, 1982, p. 120.
9 Gameson, *St Augustine*, p. 140.
10 For example Frank Stenton, *Anglo-Saxon England*, Oxford: Oxford University Press, 2001, pp. 110–11.
11 Gameson, *St Augustine*, p. 28.
12 Norman Davies, *Vanished Kingdoms: The History of Half-Forgotten Europe*, Penguin (iBook), 2011, p. 98.
13 Stuart Brookes and Sue Harrington, *The Kingdom and People of Kent, AD 400–1066*, Stroud: History Press, 2010, p. 70.
14 Bede, *Ecclesiastical History* I.32.
15 Bede, *Ecclesiastical History* II.8.
16 Richard Church (ed.), *A Portrait of Canterbury*, London: Hutchinson, 1953, pp. 43–4.
17 Richard Rudgley, *Barbarians: Secrets of the Dark Ages*, Oxford: Channel 4 Books, 2002, p. 277.

Afterword

Reflections on Leadership, Spirituality and Mission for the Church in the Twenty-First Century

In a matter of a few years, Augustine made a transition from monk to missionary, from prior to archbishop and from citizen of a dying culture to a midwife in the birth of a new nation. He initiated a missionary process, centred on the monastery as the basic unit of mission. This continued for three centuries, providing considerably more than a mere tactical adaptation of Pope Gregory's ideas into an Anglo-Saxon context.

The abbey in Canterbury and later monasteries built near rivers and the sea were chosen precisely because these places were not remote. The sea was the 'M1' of the sixth and seventh centuries and the fastest and most reliable way to travel. Roads were mere tracks and dangerous, the locals often hostile and always armed.

The scope of Augustine's mission also adapted to a changing context during the course of the journey through ancient France to England. What had begun as an initiative primarily to provide support for Bertha at the Kentish royal court through an evangelistic mission rapidly grew into a means for strengthening ties with Frankish rulers. This involved the Frankish Church in the mission to England, providing for the needs of a growing Christian community in the kingdom of Kent, developing close relationships with King Aethelberht and his court and beginning the process of reshaping the culture of the *Angli*.

Can the various strands of the Augustinian mission provide a framework for the mission of the Church today? As we look back over the past 1400 years, what are the elements, both positive and negative, from which we can learn? And which of them should be at the heart of our thinking and values, our purpose and strategy, for the Church in the twenty-first century to keep faith with its future calling and with its historic roots?

Drawing on the whole context of the mission there are lessons we can learn for our own time. Some possibilities for reflection are listed below. A relatively small number of personal and corporate 'disciplines' are necessary for effective leadership – above all, the discipline of making space in which we can hear what God is saying. These are presented through the mission of Augustine of Canterbury and draw on the vows and values that characterize the way of life of the sixth-century Rule of Saint Benedict.

Obedient Listening

Augustine became a monk in Rome. We know little or nothing about his early formation or the development of his personal sense of identity. He was apparently secure enough in himself to know what he had to offer to others. Despite his difficult task among the growing number of poor in Rome and the enervating conflict taking place with Lombard tribes during his lifetime, Augustine emerges as sufficiently secure in his own identity in God to be compassionate toward others. Asking for the wisdom and insight of others – 'obedient listening' – was less a character flaw than a willingness to learn from the wisdom that others had to offer.

Conversion of Life

The monastic vows of poverty, chastity and obedience were universal values for monks and nuns. To these, Saint Benedict added the vow of *conversatio morum,* which mainly refers to conversion from life in the world to a communal life in a monastic community. More than this, it is a conversion of heart and a discovery of one's vocation or calling in Christ, and this seems to have fallen into place for Augustine when he returned from his unsuccessful first attempt to reach England. His companions had heard that the English were strange, incomprehensible and barbaric. They feared for their lives and believed that the cause was lost; but Pope Gregory, addressing their fears through Augustine, exhorted them to persevere with the mission.

His vocation as a missionary seems to have crystallized through this episode; his own community – his travelling companions – recognized this. Augustine was consecrated as bishop in Arles at Pope Gregory's request and continued to Kent bringing Good News at the request of their own king and queen. In the spring of 597 Augustine landed in the southeast of England with the purpose of assisting the peoples of Kent in their own 'conversion of life'.

Stability

Augustine arrived in Kent with a mixed group of 40 companions – monks, priests, lay brothers and lay clerks – and began to lay the foundations for a monastic mission, clearly with the support of Queen Bertha. Augustine was a realist who possessed an inner stability and strong resolve to finish what he had begun. Stability was also a vow introduced by Saint Benedict into his community in Monte Cassino, which meant staying in the community where a monk found himself, which is essential to translate calling into action.

Augustine also knew how to separate the urgent and pressing from the important and long-term, necessary for setting the mission's priorities in a situation that could otherwise overwhelm him. He took risks in sending his two most able companions back to Rome at a critical stage for reinforcements on the mission fields of Kent.

His vocation to mission took practical expression in developing plans and priorities, particularly extending Saint Martin's Chapel, building Christ Church Cathedral within Canterbury's city wall, laying the ground plan for an abbey, and providing the monks with accommodation and the Frankish priests with a fair share of the offerings for their maintenance. A school for young Anglo-Saxon boys was established within the abbey at an early stage, and the King's School in Canterbury claims direct descent from this first school.

The mission would not have been possible without Aethelberht's baptism, his material support and protection. Augustine could not depend on increasing numbers of missionaries coming from Rome to support him; the English Church needed to raise-up its own leadership. Successive generations of monks would have been impossible without a school to educate and train the young. Following the example of Saint Benedict, who had founded his monastery near Rome as 'a school for the Lord's service', Abbot Hadrian and Archbishop Theodore later founded their own school in Canterbury to train young Anglo-Saxon boys of Kent, many of whom would take vows to become monks. Christianity in the Middle Ages was both a literate and a literary faith, and Latin was its language. Learning was not haphazard; 'entry level' was the ability to recite all 150 Psalms by heart, essential for worship, then the Gospels and New Testament and Latin grammar.

Augustine prepared carefully for mission. He had one mission programme and stayed with it for seven years, until his death. There was no change of mission strategy after three or four years; the fundamentals were put in place and then a consistent application of gospel to life and witness.

Augustine's mission strategy focused on a limited number of key areas. Firstly, on the king as the essential 'opinion leader' for his people. Working together with Bertha, the king was Augustine's first 'convert', baptized in Saint Martin's Chapel. However, without the conversion of other Saxon rulers peace in the region could not be assured, and Aethelberht became active in the conversion of other kings.

Secondly, Augustine and his companions preached to both the greatest and the least in Kentish society, the peasant farmers.

Thirdly, Christianity offered noblewomen and the daughters of kings an alternative life to multiple marriages, as one husband after another died in battle, and also an alternative to being pawns in marriages of political alliances. Several became abbesses of monasteries in their own right (as at Lyminge and Minster), releasing their considerable energies, capacities and spirituality in the service of the Church.

Lastly, there were also a few British Christians in Kent in the wake of the Roman withdrawal from Britain. They were a minority in a country that had returned to paganism, under threat and without a role in society. Some worshipped an unknown saint called Sixtus. Augustine needed to win their trust and to join them to the newly emerging Church.

These first three 'disciplines' are concerned with inner formation and spiritual wisdom, growing from dependence on others to a mature independence of thought and action when there is no one else to turn to. Augustine developed a life of praying the Psalms, not only in chapel but also out in the surrounding countryside. The fruit of personal formation is maturity and wisdom, evident in a growing inner spiritual poise and personal self-confidence. Augustine had the humility to be corrected by others when his enthusiasm for miracles seemed to imperil his soul.

Trust

A person's interior life and character soon show in public life and leadership. A good leader is also a good follower. Augustine was sent by Gregory, the Bishop of Rome, as an emissary of a worldwide Church and servant of the gospel, to the political leader of the Kentish people; he did not come in his own name nor work to his own agenda. Many have done, and history does not remember them. Together with Gregory, Bertha and Aethelberht, Augustine collaborated to shape the spiritual and political nature of the Kentish kingdom and ultimately the Anglo-Saxon world.

Augustine's inner life and public life were of one piece. He earned the trust and confidence of his new community of monks as they travelled through Francia together over nine months or more. He also gained the trust of bishops and rulers on the way, not only delivering Gregory's letters but also forging his own relationships, and called 20 more to join him in the mission. His task now was to win the trust of the English.

Vision is characteristic of effective leadership. Augustine came to support not supplant the king and queen's own vision for their people. Sent by Pope Gregory to respond to Aethelberht and Bertha's need to bring Christianity to his pagan kingdom, Augustine extended this to a vision of Christian England.

The leader of any community wins trust through a number of actions and attitudes: integrity and consistency of life (always 'coming from the same direction') and creating and energizing the 'emotional boundary' of the community. Augustine achieved this by shaping the missionaries' values and norms through a common life of prayer. They lived frugally, holding no possessions as their own, and shared with others outside their own community.

What we know of Augustine suggests how clearly he grasped this as a way of building trust. His respect for others transformed both prince and peasant. By Christmas 597 several thousand members of Aethelberht's kingdom had received baptism.

Augustine's leadership in mission was clearly different from the coercive forms of evangelism usually adopted by Rome. He showed uncommon kindness and sensitivity towards a small group of British Christians who worshipped at the shrine of Sixtus, an unknown but reputed saint in the period after the withdrawal of Roman oversight in Britannia. Bede omitted completely to mention this in his own chronicle, *Ecclesiastical History*. Augustine persuaded Pope Gregory to send some relics of Pope Sixtus in Rome to form the basis of a new shrine for these British Christians, even though neither the pope nor Augustine approved of the traffic in holy relics. This runs strongly counter to Bede's portrayal of Augustine in his dealings with the British Church in 604.

In later decades, boys who entered Saint Augustine's Abbey to be educated were not admitted to the monastic community until the age of 18, and they retained a choice to stay on as monks or to return to their families. Many chose to stay, and their vows were freely given.

Augustine also understood the use of power by observing the crucial role that rulers had in opening doors for mission to the various constituencies that comprised the community – the English Christians as well as the British Christians in Kent, pagan interests and influence – and how to deal effectively with each while keeping his own integrity. Augustine won the trust of the aristocracy, their warriors and the peasant farmers, forging good relationships with them on visits to outlying settlements, frequently with the king. This reflected how Augustine organized for mission, building an urban cathedral in anticipation of the city's renewal and growth and a peripatetic rural ministry to reach the vast majority of Aethelberht's kingdom.

Nor was Augustine slow to ask for wise counsel from Pope Gregory when he found himself out of his depth. Gregory had recognized Augustine's potential to serve as the servant of others when he appointed him to lead the mission. Augustine worked from the nature that God had given him; he could not have ministered in the way that the charismatic and extravert Columbanus from Ireland had done, or indeed Martin of Tours. What strengths Augustine did possess were enough to refound the Church in pagan Kent, and Laurentius and successive archbishops reaped the fruit of this work.

Augustine showed personal humility when he was cautioned for being carried away with miracles. At the end of his life, when he had failed to win over the British bishops, Augustine 'looked in the mirror' to find the reason for his failure. He appointed his successors and died soon afterwards, unaware of his lasting legacy.

Every aspect of their common life worked together to further the mission. The missionaries harvested their own food and gave to the poor; herbs and medicines were grown not only for their monastery sanatorium, but to heal sufferers in remote places; schools and education changed the life prospects for both women and men. When Augustine and his monks left the safety of Canterbury and ventured into the rural areas, they gave to those who were in need, they did not beg or receive. As a result, whenever they went into the rural areas, the local community welcomed them. People looked forward to their arrival, they brought Good News and were not a burden on others.

Each encounter with people was in the context of continuous prayer and chanting the Psalms, a practice that sustained the missionaries on their long journey through Francia. They spoke with the locals in the vernacular through interpreters; they did not expect peasant farmers to understand Latin. Augustine and his missionaries began where others were, asking after their religious practice with inquiries such as: 'Where are you in your practice of religion?' These practices were important for peasant farmers whose lives were dominated by forces beyond their control, forces that seemed to determine whether crops grew or cattle died, whether children lived or whether war, famine or disease swept them all away. Getting the practice of religion right was a fundamental necessity for all of life.

Core Values, Common Purpose

Augustine ensured that the right people boarded the boat with him, literally and metaphorically. He carefully selected the monks who came with him from Rome and later the clergy who joined him at Tours, knowing that their common values, purpose and attitude were essential to building an effective community that could survive and thrive in a foreign land. The monks learned the Psalter by heart. They framed their daily lives with regular worship, made prayer the basis for life and unity and dedicated themselves to living the gospel. Their life together was attractive to others who were drawn to Christ and his Church and, for some, to a monastic way of life.

As an outcome of the mission, women were also attracted to monastic life in large numbers in the following decades, living in separate communities from the monks. The culture was not yet ready for a mixed community, nor ready for women undertaking evangelism on the road. Double monasteries in England (men and women living in separate accommodation but worshipping together) were always under an abbess (such as Hilde at Whitby). The nuns, unable to share public evangelism with the monks, copied many of the books that the monks needed. Taken together, a very strong impetus for growing disciples emerged, so that at times of apostasy by Saxon rulers the peasant farmers and their families still kept the faith.

Teamwork

The fruit of the first five disciplines is the sixth. Some seeds take a long time to grow. Their support, their differences in giftedness, their capacity to learn together from experience, all take time to develop. Augustine shaped an extraordinary and diverse team whose life and ministry impacted strongly on English Christianity. He could never have achieved this alone. Nor were there solo players ministering on their own – everyone was part of a team.

The mission's church-building programme was overwhelming, engaging the whole missionary community. Augustine did not live to see the abbey completed, but others did, and that was a part of his legacy.

Renewal

The monks did not have holidays. Renewal came from a life of daily and weekly balance and rhythm, rest and learning, mission and retreat. Renewal was in the daily round, the weekly cycle, the yearly seasons. They took seriously Genesis 1 with the example of God resting after creation as a given for themselves.

The Minster Model: The Local Church and Mission

What is sometimes called the 'minster model' refers to the period when Christian ministry operated out of monasteries that, like Canterbury, sent monks to minister to several outlying communities and Christian congregations. A present-day equivalent would comprise a group of ministers (some stipendiary and others self-supporting; some licensed, some ordained, some lay) serving a local church. This unit might be a benefice, a deanery or some other similar area that has a number of locations where regular worship is maintained. The purpose is to provide a central set of administrative and teaching facilities that minister to different age groups, identified needs and missional interests.

Those ministering, both ordained and lay leaders, might also offer mutual support and commitment in terms of prayer, training and mission. Each would have the opportunity to develop a specialist ministry for the benefit of the whole locality. Discerning the gifting of each person is integral to this approach. Matters of theological tradition are respected within the leadership team, but all unite in their common understanding of the Church of England's distinctive role and approach to mission.

> The minster model is economically practical, ecclesiastically flexible, missionally nimble and culturally relevant. It involves not simply saying yes to structural change, but training clergy in theological colleges and regional institutions with the goal of preparing and training for work in this highly collaborative way as the default position to which the church is moving as a better way of doing Established Church at the local level today. Equally important, it is the most practical and coherent way of discharging the church's mission of pastoral care and evangelism to the nation.[1]

Postscript

Augustine emerges from obscurity beneath the shadow of Pope Gregory the Great as a paradigm for leadership in a new century, an inspiring figure for the leadership of the Church, the kind of leader that the world looks to for maturity and wisdom in deeply turbulent times.

Note

1 M. Turnbull and D. McFadyen, *The State of the Church, and the Church of the State: Re-imagining the Church of England for Our World Today*, London: Darton, Longman and Todd, 2012, pp. 151–2.

Bibliography

Abulafia, David, *The Great Sea: A Human History of the Mediterranean*, London: Allen Lane (Penguin) (iBook), 2011.

Alexander, Caroline, *Lost Gold of the Dark Ages: War, Treasure, and the Mystery of the Saxons*, New York: National Geographic Society, 2011.

Allen, Roland, *The Spontaneous Expansion of the Church, and the Causes which Hinder it*, 4th edn, London: World Dominion Press, 1960.

Bede, *Ecclesiastical History of the English People*, Oxford: Oxford World Classics, 1999.

Bedoyere, Guy de la, *Roman Britain: A New History*, London: Thames & Hudson, 2010.

Bing, H. F., 'St Augustine of Canterbury and the Saxon Church', *Archaeologia Cantiana* 62 (1949), pp. 108–29.

Blair, John, *The Anglo-Saxon Age: A Very Short Introduction*, Oxford: Oxford University Press, 1984.

Blockley, Kevin, Margaret Sparks, Margaret and Tim Tatton-Brown, *Canterbury Cathedral Nave: Archaeology, History and Architecture*, Canterbury: Canterbury Archaeological Trust Ltd, 1997.

Branston, Brian, *The Lost Gods of England*, London: Thames & Hudson, 1974.

Brennan, Brian, 'Senators and social mobility in sixth-century Gaul', *Journal of Medieval History* 11:2 (1985), pp. 145–61.

Brookes, Stuart and Sue Harrington, *The Kingdom and People of Kent, AD 400–1066*, Stroud: History Press, 2010.

Brooks, Nicholas, *The Early History of the Church of Canterbury: Christ Church from 597 to 1066*, London and New York: Leicester University Press, 1984.

Brou, S. J., *St Augustine and his Companions*, London and Leamington Art and Book Company, 1897.

Brown, Michelle, *How Christianity Came to Britain and Ireland*, Oxford: Lion Publishing, 2006.

Brown, Peter, *The World of Late Antiquity: From Marcus Aurelius to Muhammad (AD 150–750)*, London: Thames & Hudson, 1989.

Capelli, C. et al., 'A Y Chromosome Census of the British Isles', *Current Biology* 13 (2003), pp. 979–84.

Church, Richard, *Kent*, London: Robert Hale & Co., 1948.

Church, Richard (ed.), *A Portrait of Canterbury*, London: Hutchinson, 1953.

Clark, Peter (ed.), *Bronze Age Connections: Cultural Contact in Prehistoric Europe*, Oxford: Oxbow Books, 2009.

Clarke, Helen et al., *Sandwich: A study of the town and port from its origins to 1600*, Oxford: Oxbow Books, 2010.

Collinson, H., N. Ramsay and M. Sparks (eds), *A History of Canterbury Cathedral*, Oxford: Oxford University Press, 2005.

Cormack, Robin and Maria Vassilaki, *Byzantium 330–1453*, London: Royal Academy of Arts, 2008.

Crossley-Holland, Kevin, *The Anglo-Saxon World: An Anthology*, Oxford: Oxford University Press, 1982.

Cunliffe, Barry et al., *The Penguin Illustrated History of Britain and Ireland from Earliest Times to the Present Day*, London: Penguin Books, 2004.

Davies, Hugh, *Roman Roads in Britain*, Princes Risborough: Shire Publications Ltd, 2010.

Davies, Norman, *Vanished Kingdoms: The History of Half-Forgotten Europe*, London: Penguin (iBook), 2011.

Deanesly, M. and P. Grosjean, 'The Canterbury Edition of the Answers of Pope Gregory I to St Augustine', *Journal of Ecclesiastical History* 10 (1959), pp. 1–49.

DeGregorio, Scott (ed.), *The Cambridge Companion to Bede*, Cambridge: Cambridge University Press, 2010.

Dierkens, Alain and Patrick Perin, 'Les sedes regiae mérovingiennes entre Seine et Rhin', in Gisela Ripoll and Josep Gurt (eds), *Sedes regiae (ann. 400–800)*, Barcelona: Reial Acadèmia de Bones Lletres, 2000, pp. 267–304.

Doble, G. H., *Saint Augustine of Canterbury in Anjou*, Truro: Netherton and Worth, 1932.

Dobson, D. P., *The Archaeology of Somerset*, London: Methuen & Co. Ltd, 1931.

Donaldson, Christopher, *The Great English Pilgrimage: From Rome to Canterbury*, Norwich: Canterbury Press, 1995.

Dunn, Marilyn, *The Christianization of the Anglo-Saxons c. 597–c. 700: Discourses of Life, Death and Afterlife*, London: Continuum, 2009.

Eagles, Bruce, 'Augustine's Oak', *Medieval Archaeology* 47 (2003), pp. 175–8.

East Kent Archaeology http://eastkent.owarch.co.uk/.

Farmer, David Hugh, *Oxford Dictionary of Saints*, Oxford: Clarendon Press, 1978.

Farmer, David Hugh, *St Augustine's Abbey Canterbury*, London: B. T. Batsford, 1997.

Ferguson, Niall, *Civilization, the West and the Rest*, London: Allen Lane (Penguin) (iBook), 2011.

Fleming, Robin, *Britain after Rome: The Fall and Rise 400–1070*, London: Allen Lane (Penguin), 2010.

Fry, Timothy OSB (ed.), *The Rule of St Benedict 1980*, Collegeville: The Liturgical Press, 1981.

Gameson, Richard (ed.), *St Augustine and the Conversion of England*, Stroud: Sutton Publishing Ltd, 1999.

Gem, Richard (ed.), *St Augustine's Abbey Canterbury*, London: B. T. Batsford, 1997.

Gibbon, Edward, *The Decline and Fall of the Roman Empire*, London: Everyman's Library, Vol. IV, 1994.

Green, Michael A., *St Augustine of Canterbury*, London: Janus Publishing, 1997.

Gregory the Great, *The Book of Pastoral Rule*, Medieval Source Book, www.fordham.edu/halsall/source/590greg1-pastoralrule2.html.

Gregory the Great, *Letters*, New Advent, http://www.newadvent. org/fathers/3602.htm.

Gregory the Great, *Moralia XVIII.45.73*, New Advent, www.newadvent.org/summa/3111.htm.

Halsall, Guy, *Barbarian Migrations and the Roman West 376–568*, Cambridge: Cambridge University Press, 2007.

Halsall, Guy, *Warfare and Society in the Barbarian West, 450–900*, London: Routledge, 2003.

Haslam, Jeremy, *Early Medieval Towns in Britain*, Princes Risborough: Shire Publications Ltd, 2010.

Heather, Peter, *Empires and Barbarians: Migration, Development and the Birth of Europe*, Oxford: Pan Books, 2009.

Hill, David et al., 'Quentovic Defined', *Antiquity* 64 (1990), pp. 51–8.

Hindley, Geoffrey, *The Anglo-Saxons: The beginnings of the English Nation*, London: Robinson, 2006.

Hylson-Smith, Kenneth, *Christianity in England from Roman Times to the Reformation, Vol. I – From Roman Times to 1066*, London: SCM Press, 1999.

Jenkins, Robert C., *Diocesan Histories, Canterbury*, London: SPCK, 1880.

Johnson, Stephen, *Later Roman Britain*, London: Paladin, 1980.

Kirsch, J. P., 'Papal Regesta', in *The Catholic Encyclopaedia*, New York: Robert Appleton Company, 1911, available at www.newadvent.org/cathen/12715a.htm.

Knapp, Robert, *Invisible Romans*, London: Profile Books (iBook), 2011.

Laing, Lloyd and Jennifer, *Britain's European Heritage*, Stroud: Sutton Publishing Ltd, 1995.

Lavery, Brian, *Ship: 5,000 Years of Maritime Adventure*, London: Dorling Kindersley Limited and the National Maritime Museum, 2001.

Lawson, Terrence and David Killingray, *An Historical Atlas of Kent*, Chichester: Phillimore & Co. Ltd, 2004.

Lebecq, Stephane, 'England and the Continent in the Sixth and Seventh Centuries: The Question of Logistics', in R. Gameson (ed.), *St Augustine and the Conversion of England*, Stroud: Sutton Publishing Ltd, 1999, pp. 50–68.

Lepage, Jean-Denis G. G., *Castles and Fortified Cities of Medieval Europe: An Illustrated History*, London: McFarland & Company, 2001.

Little, L. K., *Plague and the End of Antiquity: The Pandemic of 541–750*, New York: Cambridge University Press, 2007.

Markus, R. A., *Gregory the Great and His World*, Cambridge: Cambridge University Press, 1997.

Markus, R. A., 'Augustine and Gregory the Great', in R. Gameson (ed.), *St Augustine and the Conversion of England*, Stroud: Sutton Publishing Ltd, 1999, pp. 41–59.

Mayr-Harting, Henry, *The Coming of Christianity to Anglo-Saxon England*, London: B. T. Batsford, 1972.

Moody, Gerald, *The Isle of Thanet: From Prehistory to the Norman Conquest*, Stroud: Tempus Publishing, 2008.

Morris, John, *The Age of Arthur: A history of the British Isles from 350–650*, History Book Club, Worcester and London: Trinity Press, 1973.

Norwich, John Julius, *The Popes: A History*, London: Chatto & Windus, 2011.

O'Reilly, Hugh, *The Legend of the Ermine Lady*, www.traditioninaction.org/religious/h070rp.Ermine.html.

Percival, John, *The Roman Villa*, London: Pitman Press, 1976.

Perkins, David, 'Prehistoric Maritime Traffic in the Dover Strait and Wantsum: Some thoughts as to the vessels and their crews', *Archaeologia Cantiana* 26 (2006), pp. 279–94.

Perkins, D. R. J., 'Archaeological evaluations at Ebbsfleet in the Isle of Thanet', *Archaeologia Cantiana* 110 (1992), pp. 269–312.

Philippe, Michel, 'The Canche Estuary (Pas-de-Calais, France) from the early Bronze Age to the emporium of Quentovic: A traditional trading place between south east England and the Continent', in Peter Clark (ed.), *Bronze Age Connections: Cultural Contact in Prehistoric Europe*, Oxford: Oxbow Books, 2009, pp. 68–79.

Pryor, Francis, *The Making of the British Landscape*, London: Penguin Books, 2011.

Radice, Betty (ed.), *The Age of Bede*, London: Penguin Books, 2004.

Rady, Jonathan, 'Excavations at St Martin's Hill, Canterbury, 1984–85', *Archaeologia Cantiana* 104 (1987), pp. 123–218.

Reynolds, Andrew, *Anglo-Saxon Deviant Burial Customs*, Oxford: Oxford University Press, 2009.

Robb, Graham, *The Discovery of France: A Historical Geography*, New York: W. W. Norton & Co., 2007.

Roberts, Alexander, 'Sulpitius Severus on the Life of St Martin', in P. Schaff and H. Wace (eds), *A Select Library of Nicene and Post-Nicene Fathers of the Christian Church*, 2nd series, Vol. 1, Oxford: James Parker & Company, 1894.

Routledge, Rev. Canon, 'Roman Foundations at St Pancras, Canterbury', *Archaeologia Cantiana* 14 (1892), pp. 103–8.

Rudgley, Richard, *Barbarians: Secrets of the Dark Ages*, Oxford: Channel 4 Books, 2002.

Russell, Miles and Stuart Laycock, *UnRoman Britain: Exposing the Great Myth of Britannia*, Stroud: History Press, 2010.

Russo, Daniel G., *Town Origins and Development in Early England, c.400–950 A.D.*, Westport and London: Greenwood Publishing Group, 1998.

Samson, Ross, 'The Merovingian nobleman's home: Castle or villa?', *Journal of Medieval History* 13:4 (1987), pp. 287–315.

Savage, Anne, *The Anglo-Saxon Chronicles*, London: Salamander Books Ltd, 2002.

Selected Epistles of Gregory the Great, trans. J. Barmby, in P. Schaff and H. Wace (eds), *A Select Library of Nicene and*

Post-Nicene Fathers of the Christian Church, 2nd series, Vol. 13, Oxford: James Parker & Company, 1898.

Smith, C. R., *The Antiquities of Richborough, Reculver and Lympne, in Kent*, London: John Russell Smith, 1850.

Sparks, Margaret, *Canterbury Cathedral Precincts: A Historical Survey*, Canterbury: Dean & Chapter of Canterbury, 2007.

Sparks, Margaret and Timothy Tatton-Brown, 'The History of the Vill of St Martin's, Canterbury', *Archaeologia Cantiana* 104 (1987), pp. 123–218.

Spiegel, Gabrielle M., 'The Cult of St Denis and Carpetian Kingship', *Journal of Medieval History* 1:1 (1975), pp. 43–69.

Stenton, Frank, *Anglo-Saxon England*, Oxford: Oxford University Press, 2001.

Sturgis, Matthew, *When in Rome: 2000 Years of Roman Sightseeing*, London: Frances Lincoln Limited (Kindle book), 2011.

Tatton-Brown, Timothy, *Canterbury History Guide*, Stroud: Sutton Publishing Ltd, 1994.

Thacker, Alan, 'Bede and History', in Scott DeGregorio (ed.), *The Cambridge Companion to Bede*, Cambridge: Cambridge University Press, 2010, pp. 170–90.

Turnbull, M. and D. McFadyen, *The State of the Church, and the Church of the State: Re-imagining the Church of England for Our World Today*, London: Darton, Longman and Todd, 2012.

Wickham, Chris, *The Inheritance of Rome: A History of Europe from 400 to 1000*, London: Penguin Books, 2010.

Williams, Gareth, *Early Anglo-Saxon Coins*, Oxford: Shire Archaeology, 2008.

Williams, John H. (ed.), *The Archaeology of Kent to AD 800*, Kent History Project 8, Woodbridge: The Boydell Press and Kent County Council, 2007.

Williams, Rowan, 'Relations between the Church and state today: What is the role of the Christian citizen?', 2011, at www.archbishopofcanterbury.org/articles.php/2009/relations-between-the-church-and-state-today-what-is-the-role-of-the-christian-citizen.

Williams, Rowan, 'Monks and Mission: A perspective from England', 2012, at www.archbishopofcanterbury.org/articles. php?action=search&tag_id=6&tag_id=6&tag_id=6&tag_id=6&tag_id=6&sort=date&order=desc&page=2.

Wilmott, Tony, 'Richborough, More than a Roman Fort', *Current Archaeology* 257 (August 2011), pp. 20–5.

Witney, K. P., *The Kingdom of Kent*, London: Phillimore, 1982.

Wood, Ian, 'Augustine and Gaul', in R. Gameson (ed.), *St Augustine and the Conversion of England*, Stroud: Sutton Publishing Ltd, 1999, pp. 68–82.

Wood, Ian, *Augustine's Journey*, Canterbury: Canterbury Chronicle, 1998.

Wood, Ian, *The Merovingian Kingdoms, 450–751*, London and New York: Longman, 1994.

Young, Simon, A.D. 500: *A Journey Through the Dark Isles of Britain and Ireland*, London: Weidenfeld & Nicolson, 2005.

Index